DAY TRADING
ADVANCED STRATEGIES

HIGH PROBABILITY METHODS AND TECHNIQUES TO GO ONE STEP FURTHER IMMEDIATELY AND BECOME A PROFESSIONAL DAY TRADER WITH A SUCCESS-FOCUSED MINDSET

By

Andrew Pemberton

Day Trading Advanced Strategies

Table of Contents

Introduction

Day trading is a strategy of trading financial securities, such as stocks and currencies, where positions are taken and closed within the same day. Also called short trading, it involves buying financial security and selling them before the trading day closes.

Instead of having a longer-term perspective on stocks, you'll need to reorient it to a very short-term one. In particular, you should shift your focus from a company's possible growth over the long term to its possible immediate price actions during the day.

Another area where you'll need to reorient your thinking is gains. Instead of looking at substantial gains, e.g., 10% or more, you'll need to scale down. Given the short time frame, you may have to make do with gains as low as 1% to 2%. It is because day trading involves trading at a higher frequency but with smaller gains, which accumulate over time.

You do not want to let your trade go on to the following day. It is better to cut your losses with that trade and move on, closing out the trade before the end of the day. With day trading, you are not going to make a ton of money off each trade. On the other side, the media continues to promote this trading method as a get rich quick scheme. These individuals know about the market, have a good strategy in place, and can work with the market, despite the risks.

Day trading can be difficult. They worry that in many cases, the reward is not going to justify all the risks that you take with day trading. Day trading isn't just restricted to stocks.

You can day trade currencies; you can day trade commodities as well as options. Day trading involves more of a set of practices that you stick to.

Day trading is the very definition of short-term trading. It's all about the short term because your trading horizon is restricted to one day. It means that you open a position, and you close it strictly within one day's trading hours. You engage in its daily; you focus on one or more stocks or one or more commodities or currency pairings or options.

Whether you make money or not, you are out of your position by the end of the day. That is the crucial definition of day trading.

How Day Trading Decisions Are Made

A day trader's decision whether to enter a stock or exit a stock all boils down to the probable movement of the pricing of the stock within the trading period. The trading period can be as short as 5 minutes or less, or it can be the whole day. Whatever the case may be, it doesn't exceed the whole day.

Day traders make money off volatility. They do not make as much money when the stock is trading sideways for a long time and gradually slopes up.

A stock might gain value 10% over a year, but that stock is off-limits to a day trader because the volatility isn't there. They would instead trade a stock that bounces 15% up and down, every single day. That stock has enough inherent volatility on a day to day basis for day traders to make quite a bit of money.

What Benefits Do Day Traders Offer to the Market?

In terms of economic benefits, how does day trading benefit stock trading as a whole? Well, if anything, day traders provide liquidity to the stock market. They offer a ready base of buyers and sellers of the stock. It provides the necessary movement of a stock's price that may encourage other traders to look at either the short term or long-term value and prospects of the stock. In other words, by providing action on a strictly short-term basis, day traders tend to shine a light on the overall attractiveness of a stock.

Keep in mind this is quite ironic because day traders, as a rule, do not look at the fundamentals of a stock. They don't look at the price/earnings ratio or P/E. They don't look at long term value; they don't look at industry positioning. They couldn't care less about any of that. Instead, they focus more on momentum, share movement, share volume, and price velocity going either up or down.

The Difference Between Short and Long Trade

On the stock markets, the long and short term usually means when trading begins for the first sale or purchase. The long workday starts after shopping in a store at a fixed price to sell at a higher price in the future, try to make a profit. In comparison, short transactions begin to sell before buying with the intention of his redemption at a lower market price and perhaps acquire benefits.

Short selling is simply:

- Ready for action.
- Sell the shares.
- Redemption of shares?

- Gain or loss?

The risks are also involved in the sale; stock prices can be as high, and usually, there is no limit to how a price can go. In long trade, the profit potential is unlimited, and asset prices can rise indefinitely.

Can You Day Trade for a Living?

It should be removed as it may seem, day trading is a lucrative engagement. However, this does not mean that it is like any real work. So, you have to be your boss. We will make your way at the time and their life strategies. He is incredible. Not so much happiness in this life, but also disadvantages appears. Then venture into the various advantages and disadvantages that come with day trading.

Advantages

Your Boss

Learn to work the way you want; it's always been the best thing ever; your plan, your movements, your strategies. It is so good. Imagine, wanting to go on vacation without passing first through the human resources department for a great explanation of reasons can be quite significant. On the other hand, to come work for you and gives you all the power to do things alive. It has enough minds to learn and get the best of you. Do yourself a huge favor and be your boss.

Comfort

A quiet working environment improves the quality of the final product, but rather the consequences proved to be so useful. The peaceful atmosphere creates a workspace so focused, day traders to strictly control the actual activities of daily transactions and more each day. It will ultimately achieve its critical projects identified by the large portion of the profits to realize.

Risk Management

Cases trading days of the day of exposure, without doubt, the best risk-taker. Day trading consists of many hazards, which act as day today. The merchant came to dominate the success and lay the old mistakes, to succeed as an entrepreneur.

Technologically Privileged

Day Trading Internet exposes attempts to access a variety of sources. Internet technology is full of technology. You are exposed to new places and different technological techniques. It is built because the technology is present and the future.

Cons

Solitary Lifestyle

Day trading is quiet, which means the sound of physical activity should not be part of it. This creates a kind of lonely environment, especially as the business manager, for me to try to master the correct movements possible. You can take full advantage of the trading day; the best company is usually just your business.

Incompatible Salary

Its intelligent commercial work will result in the form of compensation received by each trading day.

Decide What and When to Buy

When and how exactly to buy day, trading is so fundamental. Let the point of some of the factors to consider.

Understanding the Level of Risk Is Involved and What Level Is Appropriate for You

There are many activities for trade with idiosyncratic volatility, price, and volume. There are different types of risk experienced at all levels of daily transactions. As a beginner, choose the level of risk management of interest rate corresponding to the risk. Day of Action to the trading day, exposed to a variety of risks, which are often found in each trading day, is a learning day. Over time, a beginner is exposed to all sorts of potential hazards that can be educational, and it becomes professional risk management.

Chapter 1. How to Choose the Broker

Like with any business you choose to go with, there will be some tools that you need to become a successful day trader. The essential tools that you will need are an order execution platform. And, if you are not already part of a trading community, you may need to have a stock scanner that will help you to find the best real-time setups that will make you money. Let's take a look to see what kinds of tools you need and how you can pick out the ones that are right for you.

Choosing Your Broker

When you first get started with day trading, especially when you are a beginner, you should find a good broker. Your broker will be the one who offers you advice on which stocks to go with, and they will help you to make these orders at a reasonable price and at the right time. There are a lot of different brokers out there, and picking out the right one will ensure that you will get the best results with your day trading. Pick out the wrong broker, and you will be disappointed.

The first decision that you need to make is the type of broker that you want to work with. There are some benefits to each one, and it often depends on how much you would like to spend, how much work you want the broker to do for you, and what features you would like them to offer to you. Some of the different types of brokers that you can choose from include:

- Interactive Brokers: The first type of broker that you can choose is an interactive broker. These brokers are pretty inexpensive and can cause you a $1 or less per trade. When you are purchasing 1000 shares or more, this is a pretty good price compared to the almost $5 or more than other brokers will charge you.

- Sure Trader: This is a good option for those who are international traders and those who fall below the $25,000 minimum that is a rule for U.S. residents who want to day trade. These companies will often charge you almost $10 for completing one buy and one sell. But if you are from the United States and you do not have $25,000 available to trade, this is one of the best options to go with because they do allow you to open an account for as low as $500.

Of course, there are many other types of brokers available. Some will offer you just advice to help you get started if you just want to do the work on your own. It can save you money, but remember that you are not going to get a lot of help in the process.

One of the benefits of choosing a broker is that they will give you some leverage, about three to six times the leverage. This means that you may only put in $30,000 into the market, but you will have $120,000 in buying power (which means that you have a leverage of 4:1). This leverage is known as margin, and with many brokers, you can trade on the margin.

This can help you out if you are short on money to get started, but you have to be responsible. Buying on the margin is easy, but it is also elementary to lose all of your money as well. The margin is right because it can allow you to purchase more than you could on your own, but it adds in more risk, and you may have to pay back more money than you can afford.

If you are using this leverage and then losing money, the broker will issue out a margin call. This is a severe warning, and it is best if you just avoid getting this at all. When you receive a margin call, it means that your loss is so much that it equals the original money that is in the account. If you do not add in some more money to the account, you will get a freeze on your account.

Some will be able to offer platforms that are unique and will put you ahead of the rest of the game. Some will have different types of stocks that you can invest in, and so on.

It is a good idea not only to take a look at the different features and services that you would be able to get with them. You may be tempted to go with a cheaper option, but when you see all of the unique features that another one offers compared to that cheaper option, it may be a better idea to spend a bit more.

Trading Platform

As a day trader, you need to be able to complete your trades quickly, or you will not be successful. You do not want to be in the middle of a trade and see a big spike and then not be able to make changes or sell the stock because your platform is not the best.

There are many different trading platforms that you can work with. One option is known as DAS Trader, and it is efficient when it comes to all of the things you need to do as a day trader. Many brokers offer this platform when you are opening your account, while others will have their platform.

The best thing that you can do is check out and see how much you like the platform before you get started. You may find that you like one platform better than another based on your personal preferences.

Real-Time Market Data

With day trading, you need to be able to look at real-time data during the day. You do not get the benefit of waiting a few days or weeks for this data to come out because you need to enter and exit a trade in a short amount of time, sometimes within a few minutes of each other. There are some tools available, but remember that you will need to pay a fee, either to the platform you are using or to your broker.

Some people do not like the idea of spending more money. They are already paying for their broker, the fees they need for their platform and adding more seems like a waste. But depending on the market that you wish to trade-in, you will find that having this real-time data will help you out a bit.

It will help you to see what is going on in your market and can make it easier to adjust your trades, get out of the market when it is needed, and even to increase your profits.

Joining a Trading Community

Day trading can be a challenging thing to work on, and as a beginner, you may feel emotionally drained when you are done. And you are likely to have a lot of questions along the way. It is a good idea to join a community of traders and talk to others who are in the same boat, asking questions as needed to get the hang of things.

Having the right tools will make a big difference in how successful you can be with day trading. A good broker will be able to provide you with virtuous advice and can even help to do the trades for you quickly.

The right platform will ensure that you will be able to make the trades right when you need to. The right real-time scanner will let you catch some of the trends and keep up with how your stocks are doing. And a good community will be able to help answer any of the questions that you have along the way.

Make sure that you have some of these tools, and you will be set to go.

Chapter 2. Resistance and Support Levels

Before you can learn about resistance and support, you have to understand the basics of supply and demand. Supply and demand are the force of price movements. The market will turn up when demand is higher than supply. The market will turn down when supply controls demand.

Prices will move up when demand overwhelms supply. Buyers get eager to buy, but sellers are not eager to sell. Buyers start to offer higher prices to encourage sellers. This will cause prices to rise. Prices drop when the supply is more extensive than demand. Sellers want to sell more than buyers want to buy. Sellers will begin to lower their prices until buyers start buying, causing prices to fall.

When supply takes over demand, we can expect to see the price stops falling or rising. It will happen at resistance level support, and resistance isn't clear price levels. They happen over many different prices because most technical analysts will draw lines to show support and resistance. The drawing line showing resistance and support is useful if you can understand the lines show zones where supply and demand imbalance changes.

Many new traders don't understand how they can use resistance and support to help them with trading decisions. They understand the concept that support is when the prices stop falling, and resistance is when the prices stop going up. But making decisions that are based on these vague definitions can lead to a depleted account.

To use these tools effectively, you have to understand how prices move so you can figure out the resistance and support from the framework. There are different types of resistance and support. They are major and minor. Weak levels will get broken, and intense levels will hold and could make the price move in a different direction. By having this information, you will be able to make better decisions that are based on resistance and support.

Swing Lows and Highs

Swing lows and highs are new market turning points. They are the natural choice for finding resistance and support levels, and each swing point is a potential resistance or support level. To be an active trader, focus on the significant swing lows and highs.

Congestion Areas

Traders spend a lot of time in congested areas. They have likely formed an attachment or established interest in a price range. Early congestion areas are strong resistance and support levels. These areas reinforce the thought that resistance and support are zones and not just a specific price level. If you need to find congestion areas, a price by volume chart could help.

Psychological Numbers

Humans like to attach significance to specific numbers. Round numbers will always make the headlines. One strategy gets its trading edge from round numbers. A year's low and high price of a stock is an example of a psychologically significant number.

Calculated Resistance/Support

You can also find resistance and support from values like moving average. These work best with trending markets. Using a moving average and candlestick patterns is a trading method that uses moving average to show resistance and support.

Fibonacci retracement is a different popular method for finding resistance and support by calculations. Do having a good charting practice; you will be able to map out retracement level without having to calculate manually. Identify market swings and focus on retracement by using a Fibonacci ratio is a great option. A retracement of 100 percent is just like using swing lows and highs as support and resistance.

Flipping of Resistance/Support

Flipping is essential to resistance and support. It counts on support changing to resistance or resistance changes to support.

If a price breaks through a support level, it will show a shift of power from people buying to people selling. This support level will then turn into a resistance level that sellers know they can defend. The reverse is valid for a price breaking through resistance. This concept works with any method you use to find resistance and support levels.

Resistance and Support from a Higher Time Frame

You can find significant resistance and support levels on higher time frames before you apply them to your trading timeframe. You can take note of the resistance and support levels on a weekly chart. Then plot them daily to find opportunities. It will keep you focused on outstanding resistance and support levels and won't flood the chart with dozens of other resistance and support levels.

Trading Direction

Support levels will hold in uptrends. Resistance levels will hold in downtrends. If you see a support level holding, you should think about making only long trades. The reverse of this is true if you see resistance levels holding. Pay attention to price levels is an excellent way to find market bias.

Filter Bad Trades

The way you trade may have its way of determining market bias. By doing this, you won't confuse your analysis with resistance and support. Use your trading strategies for your primary bias. You can analyze resistance and support to augment a trading strategy.

If your strategy dictates to buy, but the price is just below a significant level of resistance, you should wait for the resistance to break out before entering pullbacks. By waiting for a better price to unfold near the resistance and support levels, you will avoid any low-quality trades.

Trade Entries

Watch for bullish signals near support levels and bearing signals near resistance levels. This is the best way to find the best trades with any strategy.

Trade Exits

Resistance and support, even minor ones, are effective as price stops and targets. The low and highs of previous sessions are essential resistance and support levels for all-day traders.

Resistance and Support is Effective and Essential

Resistance and support are features in the price landscape. Don't try to navigate prices without them.

Before thinking about any trade, map out the resistance and support levels. The zones of supply and demand will help you know the market better. Use this knowledge in your strategy to your advantage.

Ranges, Trends, Resistance, and Support

Angled or horizontal lines show resistance and support. These are referred to as trend lines. If the price doesn't move or reverses in the same area two different times without going past this level, then a line is drawn to show the market is struggling.

Within a trend, if the price is going above the highs and lows, this is creating uptrends and downtrends. Connecting these lines will make an angled line. This will show where the price finds resistance or support.

These highlight ranges, trends, and other patterns show the trader how the market is moving and what it might do in the future.

Minor and Major Resistance and Support

Minor resistance and support levels will be broken. If a price is trending low, it will make the low, bounce, and begin to drop again. This can be marked as support since the trend is down; the price will probably fall under the support without having any problems.

Minor resistance or support can give some analytical insight and trading opportunities. If the price drops below the support level, the downtrend is still intact. If the price stops and bounces near the other low, a range might be developing. If the price stops and bounces above the other low, then this creates a higher low, and this could mean a trend change.

Major resistance and support are prices that created a trend reversal. Suppose the price is trending higher and reverses to a downtrend, the point where the price change is a strong resistance level. Where the downtrend ends and the uptrend start shows strong support.

If the price returns to a major resistance or support area, the price will struggle to breakthrough. The price might breakthrough, or it could bounce in a different direction. Usually, it will retreat to a former level several times before it breaks through.

Trading Based on Resistance and Support

The primary method of using resistance and support is buying near support in chart patterns, ranges, or uptrends and to short sell near resistance in chart patterns, ranges, or downtrends.

The trend will give guidance for the direction to trade-in. If a trend is down, but a range develops, think about short selling at range resistance. This lets you know that selling short will work out better as compared to buying. If there is an uptrend and a triangle pattern develops, think about buying close to the support of the triangle pattern.

Buy neat support, and selling near resistance could pay off. There isn't any assurance that resistance or support could hold. Think about waiting for confirmation that the market is still in the area. If you want to buy at support, wait for the price to move sideways to get close to resistance or support. This will let you know the price is staying still at resistance or support. You could wait for the price to bounce off resistance or support and take the trade when that occurs.

If you want to buy near support, wait for consolidation in the support area. Then buy when the price comes above the high in the consolidation area. This lets you know that the price is still respecting the support area, and the price is moving higher above support. The same applies to sell at resistance.

If you are buying, a stop loss can go a couple of cents below the support, and if short-selling, it can go a couple of cents above resistance. If you are waiting on consolidation, the stop loss will go several cents below consolidation if you are buying. If you are selling, the stop loss will go several cents above the consolidation.

When you enter into a trade, have a price in mind to make a profitable exit. If you are buying near support, think about exiting just before the price hits a healthy resistance level. If short selling at resistance, get out just before the price gets strong support. You could exit at minor resistance and support levels.

You might be able to get more profit if you allow a breakout to happen. If buying close to triangle support, you could hold the trade until it breaks out of the triangle resistance and will continue to the uptrend. Try to exit near the resistance area.

There is a theory that old support could be new resistance and vice versa. This doesn't always hold true but will work in specific conditions.

Adapting Decisions to New Resistance and Support Levels

Resistance and support are aggressive, and our decisions need to be aggressive, too. With an uptrend, the last high and low are the ones that are important since if the price goes lower, it will indicate a trend change. If the price makes another high, it will confirm the uptrend. We have to focus attention on the resistance and support that matter at this moment.

Not resistance and support levels on a chart as they become relevant again. Delete them when they aren't relevant anymore or if the price goes through a strong resistance or support area and goes beyond it.

Chapter 3. Advanced Day Trading Strategies

Day trading strategies are vital if you want to capitalize on regular, small changes in prices. A consistent, effective strategy is based on thorough technical analysis, using indicators, charts, and patterns to predict future price moves. You will need to build a day trading strategy that fits your particular trading style and needs. Focus on the basics of day trading strategy before you get weighed down in a complicated world of highly technical indicators. Many people think that you need a highly complicated strategy for intraday success, but often the simpler, the more successful.

ABCD Pattern Strategy

By learning to recognize this setup of trading, a day trader can take action that might increase their chances of seeing a profitable return. The ABCD pattern is among the most uncomplicated and straightforward patterns for beginners to trade. There is an incredibly high likelihood of ABCD trends occurring in any stock. The ABCD pattern begins with a sharp upward move-initial spike (A), in where the stock price reaches the high of the day as buyers aggressively buy. The buyers will inevitably want to make profits, so they start selling out their shares. We end up watching the spike, and a healthy pullback follows. And once buyers overpower the sellers, a low (B) will be established as the price descends. You should not enter the trade yet, as you are not sure where the pullback will be at the bottom.

In short, we expect to split the stock above A and consider taking profit at D. When your scanner warns you that a stock is rising from A and reaching a new high of the day (B), you should wait to see if the price is higher than point A makes a support level. If it does, call that new level of support C. Then wait and watch the consolidation period. Enter trade as close to C's price as possible if the stock holds support at C. If the price goes below point C, stop the trade and exit it.

Sell half of your position when the price reaches D, and bring your stop higher. When your goal is reached, or you see the momentum fading, sell the remaining stake. The ABCD pattern can be found frequently on several heavily traded stocks. If you are trying to give yourself the best overall odds of success trading, understanding these trends will be necessary.

Why Is This Strategy so Significant?

- It reflects the traditional, rhythmic style the industry operates in.

- It looks like a flashback on the price chart that makes it easy to spot.

- It is a leading indicator for determining where and when to enter and exit a trade.

- It helps to determine the risk/reward before commercialization.

- It helps identify trading opportunities in any market (forex, stocks, futures, etc.), any time frame, and any market conditions.

Example of ABCD Pattern

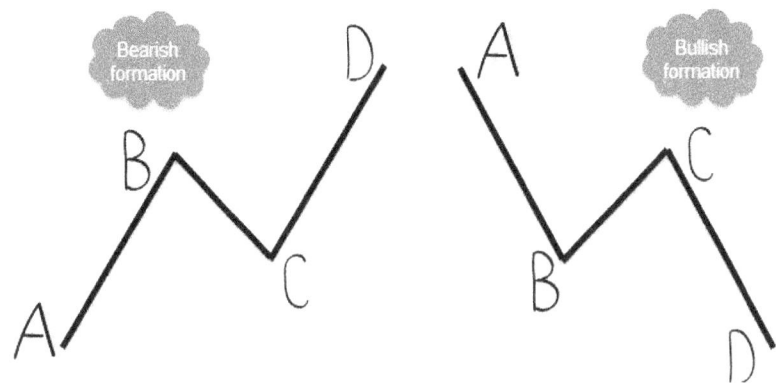

Scalping Strategy

Traders use scalping because it puts them at a lower risk and provides more opportunities to trade. Additionally, since their target is small returns, traders can combat greed. Day traders take advantage of scalping tactics. Big wins are not the aim. This form of trade provides little time for the participants to keep a stock, which means they must enter and exit the trade in a few seconds or minutes. Traders find opportunities by scanning the market for minor price changes. Prompt execution and precise timing during scalping are essential. For some traders, this trade is profitable but also puts you at risk. A scalp trader must quickly capitalize on the opportunities available.

If one of those opportunities dwindles, a lucrative trade may lead to a loss, because many scalpers will not wait for other opportunities for the same trade. That is why some people stay away from scalping because it leads to a fair extent leveraging. To pull off the most sophisticated scalping forms, you will need 1-min charts, and exchange order books.

Many scalpers do not aim to take advantage of small price movements but spread themselves on the actual bid/ask. Profiting from bid/ask spreads demands skill, and experience-scalping types are more comfortable to learn. One of the most common scalping ways involves buying a considerable amount of shares, waiting for a small upwards trend, and unloading the role as it reaches profitability. For example, a trader purchases a limit order to purchase 3000 shares at $0.95, which is the closest level of support, and if trade price falls, the trade will be carried out.

Example of Scalping Strategy

Reversal Strategy

This strategy is famous for trading because the entry and exit points are very well defined in this sense. Reversal strategy has at least five candlesticks moving upward or upward on a 5-minute chart. The stock will have an extreme RSI indicator of 5 minutes. The RSI values vary between 0 and 100. Traders in strategies for reversal use the RSI values to identify or overplay conditions and find signals to buy or sell. Your scanner or trading platform calculates RSI to you automatically. These two elements show that a stock is genuinely stretched out, and you will pay careful attention to all of these data points on your scanner.

The stock is traded on or close to a significant intraday support or level of resistance. Take reversal trades only when the price is close to a significant one. When the pattern comes to an end, indecisive candles come to the scene.

This is when you have to be informed. You are looking for either Doji or indecision candlesticks in reversal trading. They are an indicator the pattern can shift soon. In Reversal Strategies, you are looking for an explicit confirmation that the pattern is beginning to reverse. What you certainly do not want is to be on the wrong side of a reversal deal. It means you do not want to buy when a stock is selling off poorly.

Example of Reversal Strategy

Observe how it took the company two months to reach its actual breakdown from the climax of its trend.

Momentum Strategy

Momentum is a technique whereby traders buy and sell due to the strength of recent price trends. In financial markets, momentum is measured by other factors such as the volume of trading and the rate of price changes. Momentum traders bet an actively moving asset price in a given direction will keep going to continue on that path until the trend loses strength.

Momentum may be measured over more extended periods or within minutes or hours of time frames. The first step of traders is to decide the trend direction they want to transact in.

Using one of many available momentum indicators, they then attempt to set up an entry point for buying (or selling) the assets they trade. They will want to assess a viable and fair exit point based on consumer support and resistance rates expected and previously observed.

Additionally, it is recommended that stop-loss orders be below or above their point of trade entry — according to the direction of trade. This is to hedge against the risk of an abrupt reversal in price-trend and unexpected losses. The momentum indicator is a standard instrument used to determine a particular asset's momentum.

When an asset is sold, the idea behind this strategy is that the price movement's momentum reaches its height when new buyers or capital enter a specific trade. Simply, the direction of the momentum can be calculated by subtracting an introductory price from a current price.

Example of Momentum Strategy

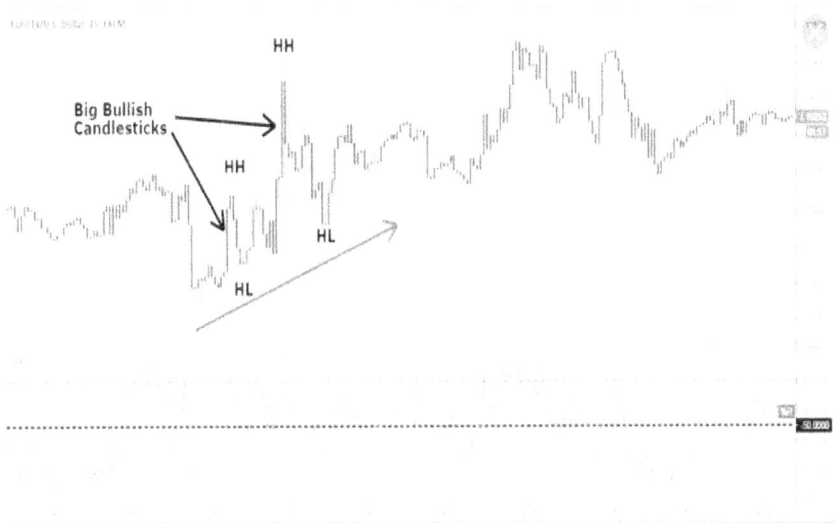

Breakout Strategy

The breakout strategy is best when the price is clear, with increased volume, and there is a specified level in your chart. After the security breaks above resistance, the trader enters a long position. Alternatively, if the stock falls below support, you will reach a short spot. You need to find the right tool for the trade. Bear in mind the level of support and resistance of the asset when doing so. The more often those points have been hit by the market, the more validated and significant they are.

That point of entry is pretty simple and straightforward. When prices are set to close, and higher levels of resistance demand a bearish position, and it needs a bullish position below the support level. To set the exit point, set a reasonable price target using the recent performance of the asset. Using chart trends will intensify this cycle even further. To create a target, you can calculate the average recent price swings. If the average price change over the last few market swings has been 3 points, that would be a reasonable target. Once that target is achieved, you can exit the trade and enjoy the benefit.The stock was in an up range in the above chart until it breaks down quickly from range to downside. If you do not watch, you will lose that quick breakout very quickly in just a few seconds or minutes. Breakouts are a vital trading strategy since they are the starting point for future increases in volatility and higher price swings.

While analyzing charts, traders can see that the period just before a breakout occurs is characterized by tight peaks and valleys, which depict a volatile market. So, a proper breakout prediction can help with successful trades. Breakouts are significant as they indicate a change in the currency pair being traded. This change in feeling can be used to make profitable trades, but it is essential to differentiate between continuing breakouts and breakouts in reversal.

Example of Breakout Strategy

Gap Trading Strategy

The post-gap trading strategy is suited for trading assets based on stocks. We will need a gap, as the strategy suggests, applying our trading rules. For this reason, we will be using financial assets that begin and end the day of trading.

These financial assets have gaps between the various trading sessions tomorrow morning. The trading session starts with a break in the morning.

Then, the trading assets will seek to recover from the craziness triggered by market opening in the next 30 to 60 minutes. The strategy suggests observing what is going on in the first 30 to 60 minutes and opening up our trading position based on these events. If the stock begins with a bearish gap and then the price fills the gap in a bullish direction in the next 60 minutes, we will have reason enough to assume that the price will continue to grow.

Another crucial feature of this day trading strategy is determining our exit points; we will constantly use price action rules. To find the best exit point, we will use trend-lines, candle patterns, chart patterns, and other on-chart formations.

We will use the volume predictor to assess the morning craziness starting, which will help us step into a steady, eventual pattern for the day. The opposite side of the gap will be an excellent place to get your stop-loss order. If you enter a bullish trade, the best place will be below the lower point of the gap for the stop-loss order. But if you enter a bearish trade, the order of stop-loss should be above the maximum point of the gap.

Example of Gap Trading Strategy

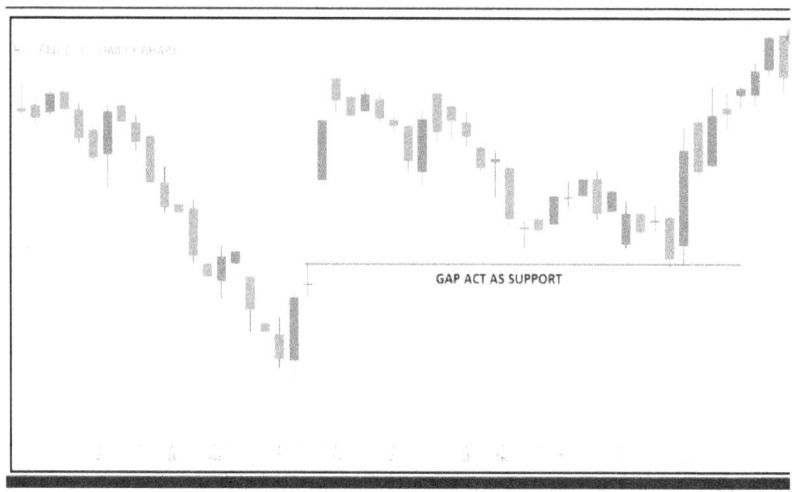

GAP ACT AS SUPPORT

Chapter 4. Technical Indicators

The Popular Technical Indicators and How to Use Them to Increase You're Trading Profits

Technical trading includes evaluating diagrams and settling on choices dependent on examples and indicators. These examples are specific shapes that candles structure on an outline, and can give you data about where the cost is probably going to go straight away.

Indicators are increases or overlays on the graph that give additional data through numerical figuring's on cost and volume. They likewise disclose to you where the cost is probably going to go straight away. Right away, here are the superstars.

Bollinger Bands

Bollinger groups are a volatility indicator. They comprise a necessary moving average, and two lines plotted at two standard deviations on either side of the focal moving average line. The external lines make up the band. Just when the band is tight, the market hushes up. At the point when the band is vast, the market is boisterous.

You can utilize Bollinger Bands to exchange both going and drifting markets. In a going market, pay special mind to the Bollinger Bounce. The value will, in general, ricochet from one side of the band to the next, continually coming back to the moving average. You can think about this like relapse to the mean. The cost normally comes back to the average over the long haul.

Bollinger Bounce, diagram by means of Trading View

Right now, groups go about as great help and opposition levels. On the off chance that the value hits the highest point of the band, at that point, submit a sell request with a stop misfortune simply over the band to secure against a breakout. The cost ought to return down towards the average and possibly to the baseband, where you could take benefits. Look at the screen capture underneath.

At the point when the market is drifting, you can utilize the Bollinger Squeeze to time your exchange passage and catch breakouts at a convenient time. At the point when the groups draw nearer together (for example, they crush), it demonstrates that a breakout is going to occur. It doesn't disclose to you anything about course so be set up at the cost to go in any case.

On the off chance that the candles breakout beneath the baseband, the move will, for the most part, proceed in a downtrend. If the candles break out over the top band, the move will, for the most part, proceed in an upswing.

Ichimoku Kinko Hyo (AKA Ichimoku Cloud)

It's an indicator that estimates future value momentum and decides regions of future help and opposition. From the start, this seems as though an extremely intricate indicator, so here's a breakdown of what the various lines mean:

- Tenkan Sen (red line): The turning line. It's determined by averaging the most noteworthy high and the least low for as far back as nine periods.

Ichimoku Kinko Hyo, outline by means of TradingView

So how might you interpret these lines into trading benefits? I'm happy you inquired.

Relative Strength Index or (RSI)

The Relative-Strength-Index (RSI). Readings more than 70 demonstrate an overbought market, and readings underneath 30 show an oversold market. Alright? Okay, we should perceive how you can bring in money from this person.

The entire thought behind RSI is to pick the tops and bottoms, to get into a market as the pattern is switching. This can assist you in taking a favorable position in the entire movie. Investigate the graph underneath.

Upturn after RSI shows oversold conditions, diagram by means of Trading View

Around Feb 6, the market was profound into the oversold domain. This is a solid purchase signal. In the event that you had purchased the market here and hung on until RSI moved over 70 (around Feb 17), at that point, you would've gotten an incredible 490,000 pips! That is nearly $5,000 per BTC!

RSI can likewise be utilized to affirm pattern arrangements. On the off chance that RSI is over the 50 levels, the market is most likely in an upturn. Alternately, if the line is beneath 50, the market is likely in a downtrend.

In the model underneath, RSI showed oversold conditions on Feb 1–2. This resembled a decent purchase at that point. In any case, it turned out the be a fake-out. Perceive how it turned out.

RSI didn't leap forward 50 = fake-out, graph by means of Trading View

At first, the value began to rise, yet RSI didn't leap forward the 50 levels on Feb 4. What's more, you can perceive what occurred after that. The market dropped like a stone, right down to underneath $6,000.

In the past case of the upswing, you can see that RSI managed to achieve 50, even though it drifted around that zone for about seven days.

On the off chance that you're more hazard unwilling, at that point, sitting tight for pattern affirmation might be the best approach. It's an exchange off between 2 things. On the one hand, you remain to make more benefit by getting into a pattern early, yet you'll additionally not be right more frequently and conceivably lose heaps of pips to your stops.

Moving Average Convergence Divergence (MACD)

This is a pattern indicator, and it comprises of a quick line, slow line, and a histogram. Have you had an espresso yet? This will be a bit of befuddling, so focus!

The contributions for this indicator are a quicker moving average (MA-quick), a slower moving average (MA-moderate), and a number characterizing the period for one more moving average (MA-period). The MACD quick line is a moving of the moving average of the distinction between MA-quick and MA-moderate. Let that hit home.

The MACD moderate line is a moving average of the MACD quick line. The quantity of periods is characterized by MA-period. At long last, the histogram shows the distinction between the MACD quick and moderate lines. Try not to stress if you don't get it the first time. We'll experience a model.

Let's assume you have MACD "12, 26, 9" (a typical default setting). It implies the quick line is the moving average of the contrast between the 12-time frame and 26-period moving averages. The moderate line is a 9-period moving average of the MACD quick line. Furthermore, the histogram is the distinction between the MACD lines.

You may need to re-read that a couple of times to get it. What's more, ensure you do get it because MACD is an exceptionally valuable indicator. So what's this "union disparity" thing about? All things considered, the moving averages and the histogram are plotted on a different diagram, and you'll see that the lines hybrid every once in a

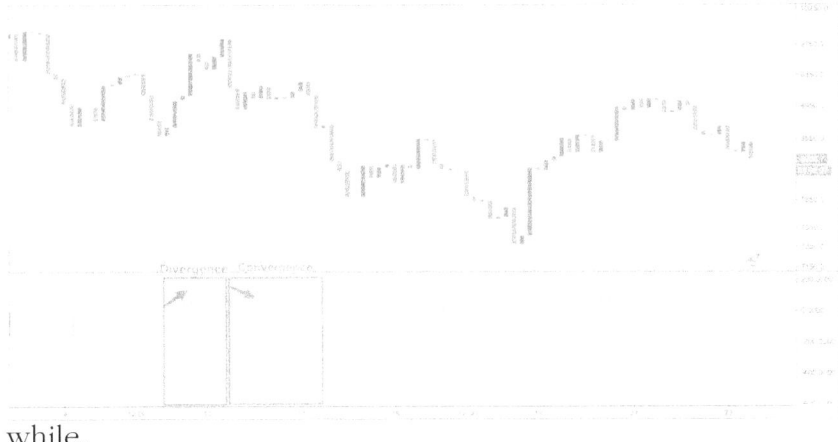

while.

MACD intermingling and uniqueness, diagram through Trading View

As the distinction between the two lines gets littler, they draw nearer together, for example, join.

At the point when the distinction gets greater, they get further separated, for example, veer. It's this attribute of the indicator that you can use in trading.

At the point when another pattern is framing, the MACD lines will merge, in the long run, they'll hybrid (demonstrating that the pattern has turned around), and the lines at that point begin to separate.

At the purpose of hybrid, the histogram will vanish because the distinction between the lines is 0.

Investigate the graph underneath

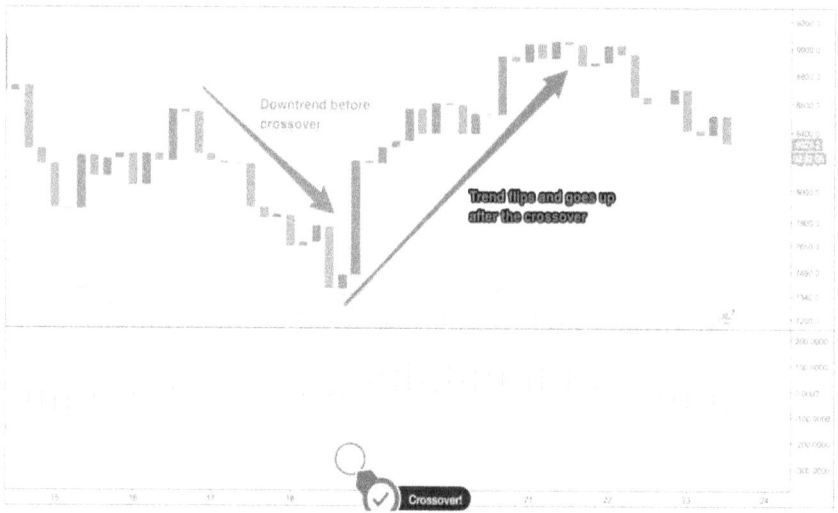

Parabolic Stop and Reverse (SAR)

Time to proceed onward to something somewhat less complex, Parabolic SAR. This is a pattern indicator. Specks are set on the graph above or underneath the cost, and they demonstrate the potential bearing of the value development. Does it get a lot easier?!

42

Illustrative SAR, graph by means of Trading View

In what manner can such a basic indicator be utilized in trading? All things considered, I'll let you know. At the point when the specks are over the value, the market is in a downtrend, showing that you ought to be short.

At the point when the specks are underneath the value, the market is in an upswing, demonstrating that you ought to

belong.

Allegorical SAR focuses, graph by means of Trading View

Try not to utilize Parabolic SAR in a running market, when the cost is moving sideways. There'll be a great deal of commotion, and the dabs will flip from side-to-side, giving you no unmistakable sign. Add Parabolic SAR to your trading arms stockpile and use it to understand stable patterns.

Stochastic

Along these lines to RSI, it's utilized to decide when a benefit is overbought or oversold. It's comprised of 2 lines plotted on a different diagram.

As you might've just speculated, stochastic can assist you with picking a passage point and get into a pattern at the absolute starting point.

At the point when the stochastic lines are over 80, the market is overbought, and a DOWNTREND is probably going to follow.

Stochastic > 80 demonstrates the overbought market, graph through Trading View

Presently when the stochastic lines are underneath 20, it demonstrates that the market is oversold, and an UPTREND is probably going to follow.

44

Stochastic < 20 demonstrates the oversold market, graph through TradingView

Indistinguishable provisos from RSI apply here. When attempting to get into patterns right on time, there will be numerous fakeouts, so you ought to be set up with stop misfortunes on the off chance that the market doesn't go your direction.

Average Directional Index (ADX)

Here's another oscillator, yet this time it's a pattern indicator. Average Directional Index (ADX) values extend from 0 to 100 and are expected to invigorate you as a sign of a pattern. If ADX is beneath 20, the pattern is powerless. On the off chance that it's over 50, the pattern is stable. Remember, however, that ADX doesn't reveal to you the heading of the pattern, only the quality.

ADX underneath 20, the cost is extending, outline by means of Trading View

When trading, you can utilize ADX to keep away from fadeouts. It's truly best utilized in mix with different indicators, as (regardless of the name) it doesn't give you any data about pattern course. Joined with a directional pattern indicator, for example, Parabolic SAR, ADX can affirm that a pattern is solid and is going to proceed. This should give you more certainty when going into a position.

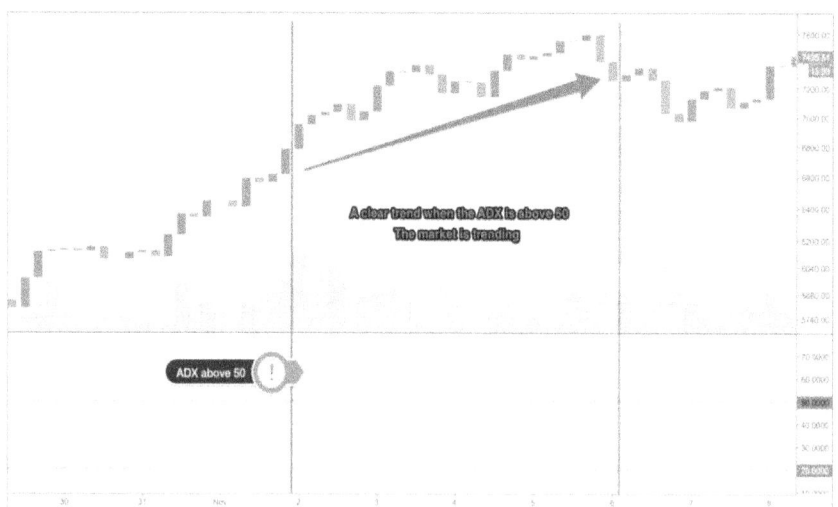

ADX over 50, solid pattern, graph through Trading View

ADX can likewise assist you with exiting the exchange when the pattern debilitates, to abstain from getting captured by value retracements.

Those are seven famous indicators that you'll see around. Make your own outlines, mess with the indicators, and discover how they work.

Know, the default parameters for the indicators may be the best for digital forms of money, or for your trading style, so transform them. Perceive how the parameters influence the signs you get from the indicators, and whether this gives you better sections, or causes you to get better patterns.

Chapter 5. Advanced Trading Psychology

To succeed in day trading, day traders require many skills, including the ability to analyze a technical chart. But none of the technical skills can replace the importance of a traders' mind-set. Discipline, quick thinking, and emotional control; all these are collectively called the trading psychology and are important factors for succeeding in the day trading business.

On the surface, day trading is an easy activity; markets go up and down, and traders buy and sell with the price. Then how come 90% of traders make losses in day trading? The answer lies in trading psychology, where most of the day traders fail. You will see many online courses advertising to teach day trading or technical analysis, but It is unheard of any course that teaching trading psychology to traders.

It is a well-known fact that controlling emotions of fear and greed are two of the most difficult decisions a day trader can take. Even those who prepare a trading plan create trading rules; find it hard to stick to those rules and plans while trading in the stock markets. It is like dieting. When you are not supposed to think of ice cream, all you can do is think of ice cream.

Nobody is born with a successful trader's mindset. It is a skill developed with practice and self-discipline. Humans are emotional beings, so it is difficult to take emotions completely out of day trading. But traders can try to remain neutral and take the help of technology to trade, so their decisions are based on facts.

But once markets open and the stock price starts changing its tracks, it sorts of hypnotizes traders in making wrong decisions. Emotions like greed and fear take over, and traders keep making mistakes, accumulating losses instead of what should have been easy profits.

In stock markets, the simplest thing is the stock price's movement. It keeps going up or down rhythmically. Any child can tell when the price is going down, or when the price is going up. Still, day traders make the mistake of buying when the price is falling and selling when the price is rising. At any given time, half of the day traders believe that markets are at a good point to buy stocks, and the other half of day traders firmly believe that it is the right time to sell.

Some of these traders are right half of the time, and some are wrong half of the time. Overall, none of them is right all the time. They get confused, not by the price movement, but by their own psychological reactions. One can easily master the part which belongs to stock markets and trading, but the other part of day trading, the trading psychology, should also be learned for succeeding in day trading.

Fear and Day Trading

The technical progress has made it possible for news to travel quickly and reach far-flung places. This has created a unique situation for stock markets, where the positive news has a quick and positive reaction in the stock markets, but negative news causes sudden and a steep drop in stock prices as traders become gripped by fear and panic.

In situations leading to greed, traders still pause and think, if they are greedy. But under the influence of fear, traders usually overreact and exit their position quickly. This has a chain-reaction effect on markets. Prices fall, traders sell in fear, prices fall further, traders sell more in fear. This emotion creates bigger ripples in stock markets than greed. Traders exit from their positions, fearing that they will lose their profits or make losses. The fear of loss paralyzes novice traders when their positions turn into loss-making.

They refuse to exit such positions, hoping for a bounce-back in markets, hoping to turn their losses into profits. What should have been a small loss eventually turns into a big one for them, sometimes even wiping out their all trading capital? A rationally thinking person will quickly exit from such a position. But fear is such strong emotion in day trading, that it stops even rational people from making correct decisions.

Technology can help traders make the right decision in such situations. Automated trading is one aspect of trading that eliminates emotional content from day trading. But automated trading software is expensive, and not every trader can afford those. So, the next best thing is to take the help of stop and limit orders. Based on your trading plan, decide what will be your trade entry, exit, stop loss, and profit booking levels. To stop you from trading before the trade entry point has arrived, put a limit order for that level. It will free you from watching the price constantly. And, if you are not watching markets always, the chance of wrong trading is also removed.

You cannot remove emotions from life. Therefore, it will remain a part of your day trading business. But you can control it by self-discipline and proper trade management techniques. Patience is also one such technique, where you stay away from trading until the right trade entry level arrives.

Greed, another Enemy

Greed leads people to day trading, and greed leads them to losses in stock markets. Traders, who are earning $1 in profit, become greedy and want to make a profit of $3. After reaching that level, they want it to reach $30. In the end, they exit with losses instead of any profit at all. Greed takes away their profits and hands them losses instead. There is another way greed makes day traders accumulate losses even after making a profit.

Once a trader makes some profit, he thinks, the next trade will also bring him profits. So, he trades again. And again, and again. By the end of the session, profits disappear, and losses remain. Then regret takes over; if only he had stopped trading after the first profitable trade. This same cycle is repeated day after day. Greed and regret come hand in hand in the stock trading business.

Greed is the most difficult emotion to overcome in stock trading. The lure of easy money, of quick profits, is tough to resist. But, like fear, traders can overcome greed by developing a trading plan and following it is strict. When a trade is earning profits, it is difficult to exit it at the profit booking level. The simple method to get over this greed is to put a stop order to exit the trade at the pre-planned level.

Over-trading is a loss-making result of greed. Traders keep buying and selling without realizing how many times they have traded or how much loss they have accumulated. To avoid this trap, trade only a few times in a day, keep this number to a minimum and stop trading ones that limit is reached. Exit the market, and do not look back. That one trade will start a series of wrong trades and over-trading. Self-control and discipline are as much required in day trading, like any other skill. Day trading tests traders' mental strength and emotional control. It may take time to develop these skills, but following your rules can help eliminate mistakes from your trading. If you reduce your loss-making habits, the chances of your profitability will increase dramatically.

Rule-Based Trading

To protect yourself from psychological risks in day trading, you must take steps to eliminate this before you start trading. There is only one thing that can protect you from the emotional rollercoaster ride in stock markets, which is a ruled based trading system.

All aspects of your day trading must be governed by a set of rules, which will involve your trading plan and trading strategies. Every day, you must go over these rules and trade accordingly.

Before you trade, sit down and think why you will start day trading? Are you going to do it for a side income? Are you going to do it for the excitement of stock markets? Or, are you going to do it to prove any point to somebody? Many traders fall into the egotistical trap of proving themselves right in trading. They will keep trading against the market and expect the market to change its course, instead of changing their trading style.

If you are starting day trading to earn a living, then this thought should always be uppermost in your mind. This should be your goal, to earn a living, and it should be your aim of day trading every day. Before you trade, remind yourself that you are doing this for a living, not for the short-term excitement. Therefore, if you make any loss, remind yourself that in business, difficulties are a part of the cycle. Try to maintain a neutral mental state whether you make profits and losses. All your trades must be made according to your plans and strategy. Before you take any trade, know the risk-reward ratio, why you enter that trade, and when you will exit the trade with a profit or at a stop loss.

Create rules about:

- How many trades will you make every day?

- What will be your loss tolerance limit for a single session?

- What will be your profit target for one session?

Stop trading when any of these three criteria are completed. For example, if you decided to take only two trades in a session, stop trading for that session once you have completed your two trades, whether your trades were profitable. If you have created a threshold of $20 loss for a single station, stop trading if you have reached that loss limit for the session. This will teach you disciplined trading, and you will consciously try to keep your losses to a minimum.

A similar rule should be applied for profit booking. Stop trading for the day if you have reached the profit target. This profit target could be in terms of a fixed amount, or the number of successful trades. For example, some traders stop trading once they have made a profitable trade.

This is one of the best greed management techniques. If you have made a profit in stock trading, even if it is tiny, just pocket it and run away from markets. Otherwise, greed will take over, and you will over-trade, trying to make more profit, and end up with losses.

Why Trading Psychology is Important

Most of the people fail in day trading because they start at the wrong end. They start by learning trading skills first and then move on to money and risk management techniques, and the last stop is to learn, superficially, about trading psychology.

The right sequence of learning day trading should be learning the trading psychology first, then money and risk management techniques and the last part should constitute learning the trading skills. It is straightforward to learn technical analysis and how to use technical indicators. But it is challenging to control one's emotions like fear and greed while trading or astutely manage money while day trading.

Chapter 6. Candlesticks

Candlestick charts are the technical tools which pack data from multiple time frames into single price bars, and for what they offer; they are more useful than the traditional. Open High, Low Close Bars, otherwise known as the OHLC or just, simple lines, which connect the dots of closing prices. Once completed, candlesticks build patterns that are capable of predicting price direction. With proper color coding, depths are added to this colorful technical tool, which can be traced back to the 18th-century Japanese rice traders.

Price Action and Mass Psychology

Price action can be defined as the movement of a security's price, which is plotted over some time. It forms the basis of all the technical analysis of a stock, a commodity, or an asset chart. For many short-term traders, like a day trader, price action has proved to be very reliable, and this includes all the formations and trends which are extrapolated from it to make trading decisions. The practice of technical analysis is derived from price action since it makes use of past prices in calculations, which can be used in informing trading decisions. It can be seen and interpreted while making use of charts to plot prices over a while.

Generally, price action is not considered as a trading tool like an indicator. Instead, it is seen as a data source from which all tools are built. Swing traders and trend traders work more closely with price action removing any fundamental analysis to focus solely on either support or resistance level or both to make predictions of breakouts and consolidation. Beyond the current price, there are some other factors that these traders must pay attention to, such as the volume of trading and the periods which they used to establish levels.

Psychology also has an impact on trading. Psychology is a critical aspect of human life, and it forms the entirety of the way humans interact with events and experiences in their daily activities. In day trading, psychology is also critical as price changes, and other market factors do not just influence the decisions of traders and investors. Psychological factors like mass psychology also contribute to the success and failure of the trader.

By way of definition, mass psychology can be described as the way traders and investors make market decisions based on emotions, news, and other resources. It has to do with following trends and conventions in the market. In the market, traders make use of data that they are aware of as well as a basic understanding of the market which they are investing in. As a result of this, markets tend to conform to average trends. Because of the psychological makeup of individuals, they tend to copy one another, and this leads to what is regarded as conventional judgment. This problem with this, however, is that humans are prone to errors, and this affects the financial market, making it somewhat inefficient.

Candlestick Charts

There are several types of bullish candlesticks: bullish engulfing, bullish harami, and hammer.

The bullish engulfing candlestick is a green candle with a large body, which completely engulfs the full range of the preceding red candle. In this candlestick, when the body is larger, the reversal becomes more extreme. The body should, however, engulf the other red candle body.

It, therefore, motivates the bargain hunters to get off the fence and move further by adding to the buying pressure. This type of candle is a sign for potential reversals on downtrends and is also a continuation signal for uptrends when they form after reversion pullbacks. The volume is expected to rise to at least a double of the average when the bullish engulfing candles appear to be the most effective. As for the buy triggers, they form when the next candlestick passes the high of the bullish engulfing candlestick.

The subtleness of the small body keeps the short-sellers in a mode of complacency as they assume that the stocks are going to drop again. Still, instead of dropping, it stabilizes before they form a reversal bounce, which takes the short seller by surprise while the stock reverses to the top. This type of candlestick is a subtle indicator that keeps sellers complacent before the trend reverses at a slow pace.

It is, however, also not as intimidating or as dramatic as the bullish engulfing candle. It is, therefore, quite dangerous for short-sellers because of its subtleness. As the reversal takes a gradual process to happen, then it accelerates quickly. When the next candle rises through the high of the previous engulfing candle, the buy long trigger forms, then stops can be placed below the lows of the harami candle.

Finally, the hammer candlestick is classified as a bullish reversal candlestick, and it is one of the most, if not the most, widely followed candlestick patterns. It is used to establish the capitulation bottoms that are followed by a price bounce which traders make use of to get into long positions. It is a type of candlestick which typically forms at the end of a downtrend to point at a near term price bottom. The hammer candle has a lower shadow, which creates a new low in the downtrend sequence and closes back up close to or above the open.

The lower shadow, also known as the tail, is expected to be at least two or even more times the size of the body. When the shorts began to cover their positions and bargain hunters came off the fence, those longs who gave up eventually are represented here. An increase in volume solidifies the hammer. To confirm the hammer candle, therefore, it is essential that the candle which comes after closes above the low of the hammer candle or, preferably, it should close above the body.

An entry that is above the high of the hammer with a long trail stop located under the body of the hammer candle is regarded as the typical buy signal. It is a wise decision to always time an entry using a momentum indicator such as the MACD, stochastic, or the RSI. Just as there are several bullish candlesticks, there are also several bearish ones. These include the shooting star, bearish engulfing, and the bearish harami.

The shooting star candlestick is classified under the bearish reversal candlestick, and it indicates a peak or a top. It is identical to the opposite version of the hammer candle. Typically, this candlestick forms following at least three or even more subsequent green candles, which points at a rising price and demand. Going forward, buyers usually lose patience, so they begin to chase the new price highs, which are part of a sequence before they get to know that they have overpaid.

As for the upper shadow, which is also known as a wick, it should generally be two times as large as the body. It shows the last buyer from the group of frenzied buyers has finally entered the stock as profit-takers also offload their positions. This is usually followed by a downward push of prices by short sellers to close the candle below the opening. The essence of this is to get those late buyers who chased after the price too high trapped.

Here, there is a high rate of fear because the exact candle which comes after is expected to close to or under the shooting star candle, and this will set off a panic selling spree because late buyers, out of panic, wish to get out to cut losses. Typically, the short sell signal forms when the low of the candlestick, which follows, is broken, meaning that trail stops are at the high of the body or the tail of the candlestick. They can, however, be signs of some very large selling activities on a panic reversal from bullish to bearish sentiments.

With the preceding green candles, unassuming buyers are kept optimistic because it should be trading close to the top of an uptrend. This type of candlestick opens up higher, giving longs to hope for another climb as it indicates more bullish sentiments at the initial stage. The sellers, however, appear dominantly and extremely bringing down the price through the first level. This stirs up concerns with the longs. As the selling continues to fall through the low of the initial close, selling continues to intensify, and it triggers more panic selling, as most buyers from the previous sales window are now underwater with their shares.

Because all of the buyers from the previous close are now holding losses, selling then intensifies into the candle close. The size of the reversal is usually a theatrical one. When bearish engulfing candles form on uptrends, they are regarded as reversal candles because they trigger more sellers for the next sales window as the trend begins to reverse into a breakdown. The short sell trigger, however, forms when candlesticks pass the low of the bullish engulfing candlestick.

Just as it is with all candlestick patterns, the trader needs to take note of all volumes, especially those on the engulfing candles. The volume should, therefore, be about two or more times larger than the average daily trading volumes to have the most impact. Algorithm programs are known to be very notorious for painting the tape at the end of the day with a mix tick to close out with an unreal engulfing candle that will easily trap the bears.

The bearish harami candlestick is the other side of the bullish harami candlestick, where the preceding engulfing candle usually eclipses the range of the harami candle completely. They form at the top of the uptrends as a result of the fact that the preceding green candle creates a new high with a large body just before the small harami candlestick is formed as the pressure of buying dissipates gradually. Thanks to the progressive nature of the buying slow down, the longs are made to think the pullbacks are a pause just before the resumption of the uptrend. The conventional short sell triggers are, however, formed at the time when the low of the engulfing candle is breached, then stops can be placed at the top of the harami candlestick's high.

There is another type of candlestick called the indecision or Doji candlestick. This candlestick is a reversal pattern that can either be a bullish or bearish pattern depending on the context of the candle before it. The candle has an identical or almost identical open and close price with long shadows. Although it looks like a cross, it may have a very tiny body. A Doji is known as a sign of indecision, but also it is a proverbial line in the sand. Since it is usually a reversal candle, the direction of the candle which comes ahead of it can be an indication of early indecision of the way the reversal will take.

Chapter 7. Keys to Successful Day Trading

No-one can guarantee your day-trading success. It is a difficult business because, from the beginning, you are up against the brightest. From my own experience as well as from many successful traders I've coached, here are five key steps that, if followed earnestly, will put you on the right path to successful trading.

Bear in mind that this is not a "get rich fast" workaround for someone new to day trading. As with most things in life, you must apply yourself to be consistently successful. To become a professional trader, find the following three points:

Having discipline in any profession but particularly in stock trading, is of paramount importance. You will need to set some specific guidelines and rules as a day-trader to follow. It's quick to get off track if you don't have clear instructions to hold in any frameworks. Anything outside of those parameters could very likely throw off your focus and cause you to make an error that you would not typically be so inclined to make. Day trading is not the kind of business one should have the attitude of "shooting from the hip" or "letting the dices fall wherever they can." If you intend to achieve some kind of income or sales targets in trading, discipline is essential.

Find a day-trading or swinging trading strategy that works well for you, and practice on that strategy until you are professional. It is important to have several approaches so that you can manage various trades as they present themselves. This might apply to trade in stocks, forex, futures, ETF, or index trading.

Learning day-to-day trade requires one to apply oneself by studying the different trading concepts and studying strategies, of course. To have any kind of success, one has to be willing to put the time in. It may be tedious at first, but when you start growing up as a day trader and experience achieving your goals, the time you've committed to learning would be worthwhile. At the end of each trading day, do a practise of reviewing your trade. This is an excellent habit of studying and everyday practice. Study and make notes about your trades. Put these questions to yourself:

Have you ever found that there is more definite energy about people who have the right attitude? People with a negative attitude exude an energy that is very different or less alluring. Which one you'd prefer to be around most? While observing positive versus negative people, a positive attitude produces more success than a negative attitude is easy to see. So you say you want to make your day-trading career a success. There needs to be a good mindset instead!

From time to time, each has a hard day. Being a positive or a negative person doesn't stop you from having a bad day. So yeah, from time to time, you'll have a poor day in stock trading or another trading strategy of the day. It is the way you approach the rough day that will decide whether or not you can resolve it. Stay positive, and you are more likely to improve your trades!

Learn How to Read the Day Trading Map

Many in the trading sector are looking to sell the latest indicator or system to you. The claims are always high, not so much as the results. You get a buying signal that last week was successful, but this time, it's not. This happens very frequently. Why that failed is unclear.

The volume shows the fuel behind the market; the price of that fuel is the result. For example, when volume expands after a long rally, but the price does not rise, it could signal that the market has reached a peak. It shows you, at the very least, that sales are flowing into the rally. None of the indicators tells you that. During all phases of a market cycle, there are specific price and volume patterns and trade setups. Learning these trends will provide you with a true advantage in trade.

Master Day Trading with Handling Sound Money

There is no trading system at 100%. Trades would still lose out. Money management lets you decide how much to gamble on each deal, and even with a series of losses, keep you in the game. It will help to define position sizing and inform the level of the stoppage. Trading success will be elusive without sound money-management practices.

Money management is more than just figuring out how much you ought to risk on any particular trade. It also contains things such as when to step up a size. For example, if you're on a trend day, you know this market has high odds of closing at its extreme. This is the time when sound money management says it puts the maximum size of your position on. Such periods will make a big difference for the week or month in which you benefit.

Develop a Plan for Trade

For professional trading business, you need a business plan. The time to figure out how much to risk when you're about to enter a trade isn't enough. Creating a proposal would go without saying you follow your business strategy.

Grasp Day Trading's Mental Game

A lot is going on 'between the ears,' which is impacting your trade. Few traders put a lot of energy into the psychological side of trading before they lose out or realize their intuition is working against them-for instance, they can't pull the trigger on a sound trading setup. Many professional athletes focus on their game's mental side, as it gives them a competitive edge. One can say the same about trading. Learn to increase your chances of success on both sides.

Trade practice

Trading well depends on the development of specific competences. How can you develop ability without putting it into practice? For an aspiring trader, simulation and paper trading are highly valuable practices. Also, traders with experience will be learning a new concept of exchange.

Honored traders remain neutral; staying impartial means being emotionally removed from your decisions on trade. I met many day traders who, after losing $100 or even less, suffered emotionally for the rest of the day, and when they made $1000, they would be "on top of the world." They do not trade neutrally.

If you're like that, then your business will be driven by fear and covetousness; if you're down $100, you probably won't want to lose, just because you know you're going to suffer emotionally. If you're up to $1000, you may want more, even if you're supposed to take profits. Or you may end up taking profits prematurely because you're afraid the position might turn against you. Professionals don't let their account faze them with the day-to-day oscillations. One week's results matter little, not even the monthly results. For beginners, emotional ups and downs are very natural.

Staying neutral also means seeing the market changes as they actually are, not just how you want them to be. You can all know the situation a trade is going against you, so you're beginning to look for other explanations why it's still a successful trade, and you should be keeping it. That's very risky as it causes people to break their stops and lose big. You have to be absolutely clear about your entry and exit criteria before you make a trade. You can still find a justification to go up or down in your place, but you no longer see the actual price change.

Change from Prediction to Reaction

Under no conditions does a day trader attempt to predict future price changes. We have to play the actual price action as traders, not what we think the change will be! Please leave the forecast to investors. They mix investing and trading. That, too, is really risky. While there may be reasons to enter a position for a short-term trade, when it goes against them, they often end up holding it as an investment. Talk of Enron, always.

Yeah, there have been occasions where trade may have been acceptable during the Enron sell-off. Even for a short recovery, I held Enron from about $8.5 to $10 the problem is, if you base your entry on the belief that the company is cheap and that it needs to recover, you'll be more and more inclined to hold or even add to your position once it goes down. The stronger your opinion about a stock, the harder it is to make decisions based on the actual movement in prices.

I would strongly advise you to have a separate, basically based trades account. You get too much leverage from a day trading account, making it very tempting to take risks that are far too high!! I'm not saying that expectations are not right; everyone should know what their future trades will most likely do. However, if those assumptions are incorrect, we must recognize that and respond to what is happening.

Not Afraid of Making a Trade

Fear or lack of faith in your trade decisions, in the first place, makes it difficult to enter the business. Often you'll find yourself letting good opportunities go by, or you're waiting for additional confirmation that the stock is going your way, which makes you trade too late, and you end up chasing stocks, often getting in at the end of the move. Fear of losing money makes it more difficult to take the losses. So much uncertainty will either cause you to take no losses at all and cause major disadvantages, or it will cause you to take losses shortly before the real stop price is reached.

Trusting in your ability to make good trading decisions will help you be patient because you know that good opportunity will inevitably come up. Traders with a lack of trust tend to look for various trading strategies whenever something goes wrong for them. So they're never able to focus on and master one strategy. Even if you're an experienced trader, you can lose some faith from time to time. Go back to trading on paper or selling small shares to get back on track.

Efficient Day Traders Use Venture Capital Only to Trade

If you're selling all the money you have on a daytime basis without getting any other revenue, you'll be far too scared to make any rational choices. There's a saying fearful money never wins. They are concentrating on a few strategies that suit them well. Many traders try to have too many strategies implemented at once. They think every day they have to make money.

The most successful traders I know have only a few strategies with which they are highly successful, at times only one. The goal is to find and master a technique that YOU are happy with. This is not going to arrive immediately. You need to look (and try) out different strategies, of course, until you find something you're comfortable with. Note that no strategy works in any market. It is, therefore, normal to sit every now and then on the sidelines. Every day you need not make money. The trick is merchandising only when the odds are in your favor and remaining in the game.

Chapter 8. Significance of Day & Swing Trading in the Stock Market

Effects of Stock Market on Day Trading

A variety of factors may influence the entry (buy) of an investor into or exit (sell) from a given stock or market. The value of scheduling the entry (buy) will vary depending on the investor and his or her priorities and timetable for investing. The tinier the time span, of course, the more important the entry is; unique entries matter little to long-term depositors.

That being said, all investors should be conscious of some of the more popular moving market forces that can disturb the price of a stock. In being aware of these business subtleties, buyers will make better investments and, in return, capture an extra or two percent. Let's look at the eight variables that can have a significant effect on the typical trading day.

Foreign Market Place

The NY Stock Exchange opens at 9:30 am for exchange every single day. Before the "Big Board" opens trade, stock markets in Asia and Europe have already (or nearly) ended their trading day. The fact is, if some stocks or industries have a predominantly good or poor day in those markets, the Feeling could have a consequence on exchange here in the U.S. A negative outlook for technology firms in Asia or pharmaceutical corporations in Europe, could effortlessly tumble over into U.S. trading and trigger American technology and pharmaceutical shares to take a descent.

This fact has considerable adverse effects on all the big indexes. When you see big negative activity impacting your segment in a foreign market, it may be healthier to wait until the dust relaxes before you get into place. This would save some of your money right from the beginning.

Financial Data

If around is talk of China being able to reevaluate its currency (the yuan), then it will cause outside exporters to China to trade higher stocks of exporters. (The reasoning behind that is that more U.S. - made goods with a higher yuan would be available to Chinese companies and individuals).

Parenthetically, increases in interest rates may also cause liquidity to drift into or out of major markets. For instance, if U.K. interest rates Upsurge, investors can escape for healthier opportunities in that market. U.S. firms will often gain the benefit.

When you made your decision to invest, you should be mindful of any financial news that comes out or will come out when you go into your place. If a highly predicted economic release is about to surface that could result in market unpredictability, it may be paramount to wait for its announcement rather than jumping in early.

Futures Statistics

While a person may be prepared for securing or sell "available" stock at a sensible price, upcoming data may offer the individual a better indulgence of whether that would be possible in authenticity. Index futures represent the most significant market directories. They start interchange beforehand the stock marketplace and are a very decent pointer of what it will sense like to open up the stock market. This is for the reason that index futures values are closely connected to the actual point.

In short, depositors will search to see if futures indentures traded in premarket interchange are higher or lower. It would give them a stronger sense of where the directory they are looking might be shifting "after the break." Normally you would hear CNBC or other market sources reporting about DJIA or S&P 500 futures activity before they break.

Purchasing At the Opening

It may not be a good impression to purchase or sell stock at the opening of the market. Why?

Usually, a lot of purchasing and retailing occurs throughout the first hour of the interchange day. Essentially, the opening hour of exchange is the first time most market members have to join or leave the stock, and can easily produce higher than the regular capacity of trading. Many market members respond to the innumerable news items that seemed between the concluding of yesterday and the opening of today, containing major market news proceedings such as economic developments and political shifts.

A handful of bellwether inventories announce earnings or distribute news before the open. This can cause some depositors (both retail and institutional) to move wealth at the first chance they get in or out of a zone — creating crazy haste at the open.

Noontime Trading Pause

Usually, there is a reduction in trading (meaning the trade capacity) at noon because the majority of the big news proceedings are out of the marketplace. Stock values can also drop some ground during this break. When this occurs, stocks can be bought at 1 pm at a low price than purchased at 11 am. It is significant to study once again because this can influence both admission points and departure points.

Analyst Assessments

An analyst can publicize an intraday memo that can disturb a given stock or subdivision significantly. As a landfill, do not overlook to check monetary websites or watch TV publicity videos. When a big company has either been promoted or downgraded, seek to determine the possible effect on specific markets and the economy as a whole.

For example, if a well-known analyst demotes a big stock of semiconductors due to slackening requests for goods from that firm, it would be fair to conclude that other smaller players would experience similar trends. It may also be rational to believe that stocks of computer makers (which buy large amounts of semiconductors) may also be affected.

Also, if a significant homebuilder has been promoted due to specific requests for their homes, it is fair to believe that other prominent players in the industry (who have the same physical footprint) will experience similar requests increases. By definition, rising demand for new homes may mean a significant opportunity for home development stores and furniture manufacturers.

Social Networking and Blogs

The internet has altered how people participate, as well as how the general community gets news; therefore, whether a web author or reporter spreads a bullish or bearish article about business throughout the day of exchange, it can have a major consequence on their stock.

All investors will endure to search the web and visit main news sites during the day to see if the public domain has any potentially market-moving news articles. Be vigilant about avoiding sites offering endorsements based on the shares they own. Such pump-and-dump schemes predominate on the network.

Friday Exchange

This means that stocks during the last few hours of the trading day can and frequently sell-off Friday afternoon, if for no other cause than traders are looking to go home "square" (without positions on their books). Keep this in observance when trying to find an appropriate time to join or leave a stock place on Fridays.

Although company-specific incidents can impact stock prices, there are a variety of other variables that can also impact the shares. Savvy investors will know it.

What to Aspect for In a Day Exchange Stock

With thousands of stocks to select from, how will you determine which ones you will be concentrating on for day trading? Trying to find it out can get complicated. Every day, some traders discover new stocks to sell, or look for stocks that fall out of trend. Many watches for stocks that break out, or are the most unpredictable, of support or resistance rates.

Many traders are examining for increasingly unpredictable stocks, selling a few of such stocks for weeks on end. There are also those who merely regularly trade the same one or two stocks.

This last strategy is more advantageous to day traders as they are less research-intensive—day traders do not need to continuously locate new stocks, or check for instability and breakouts. When you are one of these traders and want to trade one or two stocks (or ETFs) consistently, there are a few considerations that can help you determine which stocks to choose from.

Capacity

An active day trader needs an appropriate amount of stocks to enter and exit trades on request. The larger the number, the simpler it is with little to no slippage to enter and exit positions (relative to smaller number stocks). Slippage happens when the price of the sales order or stop-loss varies between the time the order is issued, and when the transaction occurs. This is usually in circumstances where orders are higher than the average number of a bid or offer shares.

Although tastes vary, traders on several days will exchange stocks with a regular amount of at least 1 million (often several million) trades. Some of the most widely traded securities in the U.S. is an exchange-traded fund (ETF)—the S&P 500 SPDR (SPY)—which has a steady capacity of about 95 million. A portfolio screener will help you narrow down the number of stocks to an amount that you can handle. If there are still plenty of stocks in the list, work to minimize them by just considering stocks in a regular average volume that do 3 million (or more).

Instability

A growing day-to-day trading approach is to trading stocks that are rapidly moving all day. Every stock has a different "personality" unpredictability. Some stocks will move around 0.5 percent per day on average, some move around 1 percent per day, and some stocks exchange more than 5 percent per day.

Whatever stocks you want to trade depends on your business style, reflexes, broker, and personality. Most people find it tolerable to trade a stock that moves 0.5 percent to 2 percent per day while considering a stock's major swipes that move 5 percent per day difficult to deal with.

Many people are not mentally or bodily sufficiently supple to respond to a large number of unstable stocks and the price variations they may undergo. This will impede the successful execution of trades in stocks with higher instability.

To make it more manageable, a stock screener (such as Finviz) may be used to thin down the number of pillories to a size that's good for you. When after the reduction, there are still a lot of stocks on the list, seek to minimize the size of the list further by only bearing in mind stocks that shift in small amounts, such as 1 or 2 percent.

A few day traders can even opt to sell stocks on news that moves a stock significantly. Such are called impact stocks, which can deliver uncertainty as a competitive advantage.

Trend or Assortment

Other factors to ponder are the trend and assortment of investments. There are a variety of traders, trend traders, and others who are effectively doing both. Scope refers to the difference between low and high prices of a stock in a given exchange period, though trend denotes the general way of the price of a stock. The prices may shift up or down uninterruptedly, suggesting an uptrend or downtrend.

A stock screener will help you classify trends or variety stocks, and you'll still have a list of stocks to apply your daytime trading approaches. It will take some effort to find stocks that agree to your trading system, as the crescendos within stocks shift over time. However, time is well spent, since a technique implemented in the right context is far more successful.

Chapter 9. Trading Order Types

Investors are utilizing a broker to buy or sell an asset utilizing their option of the order form. They initiate an order once an investor has decided to buy or sell an asset. The order gives guidance to the broker regarding how to proceed.

Commercial securities are usually traded through a mechanism of bid/ask. A buyer is willing to pay the price of selling must be present to sell is meant by this. There needs to be a ready seller to offer as the price of the buyer to purchase. No deal happens when a buyer is there, and the seller is also there. The offer is the highest price advertised that someone is ready for asset pay, and the request is the lowest price advertised at which someone is ready to asset sell. The changes in the bid and the ask are constant, as each offer and bid represents some order.

The rates can change when commands are filled out. E.g., if a 25.25 bid is there and another bid of 25.26, the next highest bid is 25.25 when all 25.26 orders have been completed. This process of bid / ask is a key to remember when an order is placed, as the selected order type will affect the price at which filled the trade, when it is going to be filled out, or whether it is going to filled out at all.

Types of Orders

Orders are taken in most markets by the individual as well as institutional investors. Mostly by broker-dealers, individuals trade that requires to place many types of orders when doing business. Markets facilitate various types of orders which provide some discretion to invest when planning a trade. Some basic types of order are as follows.

- Order of the market shall instruct the brokerage in order completion at the price available next. Orders of the market have no fixed demand and are usually performed on all occasions when there is little competition in the exchange. Orders of the market are typically used when the trader wants the trades quickly in or out, and the price is not the concern they are getting.

- The brokerage is instructed by the order cap to acquire at or less than a defined amount, the security. Limit orders make sure a customer just pays a certain security purchasing price. Limit orders may remain effective till executed, expired, or canceled. A broker is instructed by the sell limit order to sell at a price above the price currently, the asset.

- Such a form of order is used for long positions to gain gains as the price rises higher since purchasing. The brokerage is instructed by order of sell stop to sell if the asset is or reaches a price less than the price currently. An order of buy stop may tell the dealer to acquire an asset until it hits a level above the amount currently.

- An order of the market is the stop order meaning that once triggered, and it can take any price or order of stop limit it can be and where it can be only executed within a given limit (price range) after triggering. Day order shall be conducted on the same business day on which set the order. Good until orders cancelled remain effective till they have been filled or cancelled.

- If the order isn't an order of the day or good till the order has been cancelled, the trader sets the order expiry typically. You must complete a kill or fill orders quickly and absolutely or not completed at all.

Trade results are affected by these kinds of orders. For example, a buy limit placing at a price lower than the asset is currently trading can give a better price to the trader if it decreases the asset in value (in comparison to now buying). But holding it so low will imply that never the price hits the limit value, so if it falls higher the price, the trader can lose out. One type of order is no better than the other. That order style serves a function which, in various cases, would be the correct alternative.

Order Usage for a Trade of Stock

A trader will think about how they are going to get in while purchasing a product and how they're going to get out on both a loss and profit.

This means that potentially three orders there are that at the beginning of a trade can be placed: one to enter, one to control the risk if does not move the price as expected (as stop-loss referred), and other to trade profit eventually if the price moves in the direction expected known as a profit target. An investor or trader should not position their orders of withdrawal at the same moment as they start a deal, but they will also be informed of how to get out (with a profit/loss) and what forms of instructions they should use for doing so.

Suppose a broker decides to buy AAPL (Apple Inc.). One configuration that can be possible is here that they use to place their orders for business and also control risk and have profit.

78

We track an exchange alert technical indicator and then put a trading order for buying the product at 124.15 dollars. The order will come in at 124.17 dollars. The disparity in the quality of the sales order and quality of the fill is known as slippage. They agree they do not want to gamble higher than 7 percent on the product, so they placed an order of sell stop at 115.48 dollars, 7 percent below the entry of them. That is power over defeat or failure end.

On their study based, they conclude that they should make a trade benefit of 21 percent, which implies that they intend to lose three times. That is a strong ratio of risk/ reward. They, therefore, place an order of sell limit at $150.25, which is 21 percent above their price of entry. This is the target for profit for them.

First, an order of selling will be there, by which the trade will be closed. In this scenario, the price first reaches the limit of selling, results in a profit of 21percent for the trader.

Market Order Definition

An investor's bidis and order of market –usually made through a brokerage or service of brokerage – for buying or selling a stock at a price best available in the present market. The most reliable and fastest way of entering or exiting a trade is considered widely and gives the best way to get in the trade or out of it quickly.

Business orders virtually instantaneously step in for other liquid stocks large-cap. Of all the orders, the basic most are considered market order. It is intended to be implemented at the existing selling price for defence as quickly as possible. That's why other brokerages have a button of Buy / Sell trading apps.

Typically perform a business order by clicking this switch. In cases, mostly market orders experience any type of order lowest commissions, since either broker requires very less work.

Key Takeaways

- A market order is an investor's request for security buying and selling.

- Large price instruments like large-cap options, derivatives, or ETFs are well adapted.

- An order of market will be executed by the trader if he/she is ready at the requested price to buy or at the requested price to sell.

When Market Order be used

For securities traded in extremely high volumes like stocks of large-cap, ETFs or futures, market orders are well suited. For E-mini S&P, the orders are market.

For example, a stock like Microsoft tends very quickly to fill without issue. Of stocks with weak floats or limited total regular value, this is a different matter.

As such, stocks are traded thinly; the distribution of the asking bid appears to be large.

Due to this, market orders are sometimes slowly filled for securities like these and at prices unexpected often, which leads to significant trading costs.

Slippage of Market Order

It implies that if a dealer wants to fulfil a trading offer, the seller can purchase at the selling price or sell at the price of the bid. Thus, the market order executing guy leaves the asked bid spread immediately.

For reasons like this, it is the best idea sometimes to take a close look at the spread of the asked bid before an order of the market is placed– especially for securities traded thinly. Failure to do so could incur very high costs. It is doubly relevant to the individuals also who regularly deal, or whatever utilizes an electronic training program.

Market Order vs. Limit Order

The basic most buying and selling trades are market orders. Also, on the different side, limit orders allow the investors more extra price control of bid price or price of sale. It is achieved by specifying a maximum reasonable value of the sales price or an appropriate minimum acceptable price of sale.

The ideal is the Limit orders for trading thinly traded stocks are volatile highly or have larger asked bid spreads.

Market Order Example of Real World

Assume the asked bid production costs for Excellent Industries shares are respectively 18.50 dollars and 20 dollars, with hundred shares available on request. If the trader places an order for buying 500 shares on the market, at 20 dollars, the first hundred will execute.

Nonetheless, the upcoming 400 fill up the upcoming 400 securities at the highest selling price for sales. If traded the stock very thinly, the upcoming 400 shares could be executed around 22 dollars or greater. This is exactly why the usage of limit limits for such forms of shares is a smart idea.

The market orders trade-off filled at a dictated market price in opposition to restricting or stopping orders, which give more control to traders. Sometimes the use of market orders may result in unintended or significant costs in some of the cases.

Chapter 10. Common Mistakes to Avoid

It is necessary to be using the right strategies to have success, but it also necessary to know what not to do and what mistakes and traps you should avoid. Below you can read about common mistakes that many traders have committed before so that you can learn from them and avoid them. You should attempt to incorporate all of these mistakes into your strategies somehow so that you can avoid them.

Never buy assets without having a plan beforehand, don't just hope that the price of an asset will go up after you buy it since this is rarely the case, and you can't rely on the luck long term since it tends to catch up to people. Enough beginners have already fallen for this mistake, and they will get emotional when the reality slaps them in the face, and the price of an asset starts going down. They get emotional, and they start hoping that the price will continue to go up for which there is no guarantee. This is an example of a sunk cost fallacy where it's hard to walk away from something that a person is invested in, monetarily or emotionally.

Another variant of this mistake is when the price of an asset is going up, and the trader doesn't want to sell since he or she wants to hold out for more, and that happens to come back to haunt them when the price inevitably starts to go down. The plan will make it at which price it is necessary to get out of a trade and how much risk tolerance is allowed.

The plan will necessarily provide a trader with clear points of entering and exiting a trade, and a trader has no business going into a trade without a plan.

Another unfortunate mistake does not know when to cut costs, and this is a mistake that probably costs traders the most money out of any other mistake. This fact is generally a universal human problem since it takes a lot of humility to admit when someone is not right. You won't be on point with all your trades, and that is fine, and that is just how it goes. You just need to be right more often than not.

It is necessary to recognize when you are not right and to get out of a bad trade pretty damn quickly. You should have a plan and a course of action for exiting a trade, and you also need to be aware of an acceptable amount of risk to be taken. You should know if the potential reward is worth the risk, and once you are a particular trade, it is necessary to stick to a plan.

It may take some time to get used to the fact that you will have to determine how much loss is too much, even if a trade looks perfectly fine on paper. It may be a bit unintuitive. It can protect you from a lot of pain and losses further down the road. You don't want to commit a mistake of buying stocks that don't provide you with information about their volume since this is one of the key pieces of information along with the price to which you should be paying attention. Don't just look at the price; you don't want to be one-dimensional with decisions such as these.

Don't pay attention to stocks that aren't backed by a lot of volumes and you will have to pay close attention to identify stocks that have volume since this isn't something that you can determine by simply glancing at the price since price can rise nicely even without the volume being present. The price can't really raise all that significantly if there is no volume to support that increase, and for that reason, you never want to be too quick to jump on a certain stock.

You should be keeping some form of a trading log, and this is what will set you apart in terms of your results, and you should be keeping a journal when it comes to every single trade, no matter how good or how bad the trade may have been.

What you should be noting down in your log are your strategies and your approach for each trade, and you should also capture what you were thinking when entering a trade and what were your reasons for entering and exiting a trade. You should also include details about the timing of entering and exiting trades. As Peter Drucker said: „What gets measured gets accomplished. " This will essentially allow you to learn from your experience, and this is how you will get better.

This mistake is even more crucial to avoid for those that aren't starting out with a very sizeable amount of capital. This is an impatient mistake, and you should be thinking about the long term and doing things that will ensure that you achieve long term success. No matter how attractive a certain trade may look, you don't want to forget about a plan and the rules of the plan. Stick to the plan and your risk management strategy and think before you leap. Don't put all your eggs in one basket.

If there are certain things that you want to test out, always do it with a small sample, and never in a trade that is a real deal that is a rookie move. Once you start getting more success, and you know how to replicate that success, then you can slowly start increasing the size of the position.

Another mistake is placing way too much trust in intermediaries. Intermediaries such as stock promoters have their plan, and they want for the trade to go through so that they could get their commissions even if the particular trade may not be the best choice for you personally.

Another mistake is trying to reinvent the wheel and trying to trade based on the patterns which aren't even on the chart you are convinced are there. The things on those charts, which will be a basis for your decision, should be clear and unambiguous. This is what will, without any doubt, show you what is actually going on in the market, and it is not necessary to reinvent the wheel here. It is necessary to take a step back and just to realize what is there and if you should go forth with a particular course on action based on what you are seeing.

The next mistake you should avoid is not paying attention to all the indicators, and you should be paying attention to them since you will be able to gain much insight about a certain asset if you can read between the lines. If you know how to read indicators, then you can recognize when a certain uptrend is coming to a close, and that should be a signal for you, as a trader, to pull out and take your profits with you. Listen to the indicators to know when to get out and also when to stay away from a certain asset.

The next mistake is getting emotional and making decisions based on that. You should be able to keep a tight enough leash on your greed and your fear so that you wouldn't be committing all sorts of mistakes that could have been avoided by simply slowing down and observing how things are. Emotions don't have to be a bad thing necessarily; you can productively use them if you can control them.

Fear can also be used more constructively since fear does exist to keep us away from harm, and fear can be your friend when you want to avoid getting into bad trades that won't go anywhere. Fear can make you more smart and cautious to a certain extent, and it can save you a lot of money. You want to maintain your composure and always to know should you be bullish or bearish in a certain situation. Always try to take a moment and a step back before making important decisions.

Another mistake is playing by the ear and trading based on your gut, and you definitely shouldn't be entering a trade just because it feels right. You should be making your decisions on the basis of cold hard facts. You should know which things on charts are worth paying attention to when looking at the charts and in this way you will be regularly buying assets that are going up and selling those that are on their way down.

You should also be keeping a mistake journal in which you will be noting down all your mistakes and lessons gained from them. You need the discipline to stick to your plan, and that is how you succeed. You should also be sure that you are ready and that nothing is left to chance before entering a trade. Know which criteria are essential and focus on those before entering the trade while ignoring the unimportant stuff.

When you set a stop order, you should take it seriously and stick to it. This is how you will save a lot of money down the road during your day trading journey. It is necessary to know when to stop when you are doing well, as well, so that you could take with you as much profit as you can. Stop rules are what you need to stay focused on the current trade and not to get distracted all the other shiny and fresh opportunities.

When the price starts to fall, it can fall quickly, and that is why getting out at the right time is so crucial since you risk losing your profits pretty quickly. Your orders for stopping a trade should be active and ready for implementation as soon as possible. You should also be aware of how risky the trade is and how much risk you are ready to undertake.

The final mistake is not being adequately prepared before going into the trade. You need the discipline to succeed, and you need to stick to the systems that you have set out for yourself. I realize that you are probably doing day trading because you want to be your own boss and to have the freedom, and that is great, but to succeed with that, you will need to have discipline, and you will need to follow your own systems. It is necessary to work now and to sacrifice a bit of fun to be able to reap the rewards in the future. It may not be fun at the moment, but it will be all worth it in the end. You should be keeping a log, and in this way, you will know what is responsible for the majority of your successes and ditch the strategies that didn't bring you a lot of good.

Chapter 11. Day Trading Myths

Day trading is possibly one of the most popular types of trading today. You may have heard about it from a friend or seen a good video online. And like so many trending topics, there are many common misconceptions about day trading, let's try to dispel some of these myths right now. As a concerned day trader, I know you have heard a lot of day trading myths, but it's best to stick to the facts. Here are the most famous myths about day trading today.

Myth #1. Day Trading Is Like Gambling

If I hear someone else say this, it could make a hole in my drywall. Day trading is the farthest thing from gambling. Like anything in life, if you take something and are not prepared, you will make sure you know what has been delivered to you. Day trading requires tremendous practice, attention, and dedication to a tot of rules. If you upkeep your eyes on the ball, day trading can be as predictive as receiving a paycheck every two weeks from work.

Myth #2. Daily Trade Is a Man's Game

Trade is in no way man-oriented because we are perceived as hunters and the latest competitive creatures. Some of the best traders in the world are women.

Myth #3. Arrests Are Not Necessary

I set to work with the idea of trading without interruption. My premise was that using stops was a glorified way of saying that you were too scared to risk your position. ! Wrong you should use stops to make sure you don't lose all the capital on bad deals.

Myth #4. You Can Earn Money by Trading All-day

This is a bit of fact and fiction; however, I will say that the majority of day traders exchange money in the morning. Since this is not about playing on both sides of the fence, then I must say that it is a myth to think that you can trade all day and constantly make a profit. If you're overcoming weeds over lunch, you will literally go nuts as you watch the rapes stop, and the low-altitude trades push a title in one way or another.

Myth #5. Using Margin Four Times Is a Good Idea

Margin is purely psychological for most traders and has little to do with managing risk or hedging a position. Traders only see that they can use four times their margin, so they launch their funds to the market. As a trader, you will soon realize that more margins you will eventually use will prove disastrous as you go through an expected recession. Margin should be used wisely, and maximizing margin is never a good idea. In life, you should always keep a hatch open in case you need to take a last-minute vacation.

Myth #6. Premarket Trading Is Profitable

Trading is scheduled between 9:30 a.m. and 4:00 p.m., trying to dominate the pre-market business domain somehow to anticipate that the market is a sham. Volumes are small, and supply/demand spreads are dire. Focus your efforts on trading during key market hours.

Myth #7. After-Hours Trading Is Profitable

The same rules apply to traders trying to jump into the pond before the market opens the next day.

Myth #8. Day Trading Futures Is Easy Money

Futures trading is more complicated than stocks, in my opinion. Multiple professional traders trade no wonder futures with a hyper-focus on one or two instruments (E-mini, etc.). You'd better compete with retail stock traders until you get your feet wet.

Myth #9. You Need Tons of Daily Business Monitors

Save it. Don't go out buying a custom trading setup of the day because you have to see six different time frames for the same stock. If you can't understand the action with three monitors, you definitely won't be able to understand things with 10.

Myth #10. You Can Exchange a Day From Work

A day from work is a horrible idea. Unless you're working on a server farm and things never end, daily distractions at work will compromise your business performance. Not to mention the fact that your employer is paying you to work, so too bad. Let me not judge, but you understand.

Myth #11. There Is Money In the First Thirty Minutes

There is a lot of money in the day trading in the first 30 minutes. Sad for you, it is really difficult to make a profit constantly. It will take years, and I mean years of business experience so early in the morning before you can identify trends to make decisions in a fraction of a second. The market is not forgiving in the morning, so if you don't know what you are doing, volatility will kill you.

Myth #12. Let Your Winners Run

For beginning traders, they will interpret this to mean holding on to my titles forever, because they will flee to the moon. So, let your winners get to a certain point, but you have a plan for when you need to get out of your position.

Myth #13. You Have to Sell Half of Your Position Once It Is a Little Higher

Some traders sell half; I am still selling my entire position. I noticed that when I sold half a position, I relaxed my rules and got a little sloppy in the second half. So, I just make more money when the pressure is on me, and I'm on the ball. So, focus on trading the entire position and leave multiple entry/exit strategies to people trying to overcomplicate the market.

Myth #14. The More Indicators, the Better

Show me a trader with ten or more indicators on your chart, and I will show you a broken trader. Adding a million markers to a chart will not correct the fact that you have no idea what you are doing. Don't get in the way with confirmatory and contradictory views. Have enough courage and self-confidence to have what it takes to be successful in day trading.

Myth #15. Daytime Trading Fees Are too High

One-day trading earnings are taxed on any income tax bracket you re-enter. Stop thinking that the man is willing to take 50% more of your commercial profits. Remember, paying taxes is something good; it means you are a profitable trader.

Myth #16. Day Trading Tips Are Helpful

Day trading tips are one of the most damaging things you can expose yourself to in the market. If you find yourself on cruise ship pick sites and social sharing sites, stop.

You'll never get people to fill up on the board, and you have no way of knowing what's going on behind the avatars.

As far as you know, the forum member might say to sell, when in fact, they hope to get the shares at a lower price. Remember, you are dealing with trades, and these are not always good people.

Myth #17. You Can't Trade from a Laptop

There are now tons of traders traveling the world and continuing to trade on the go. They just take out their laptop, load up some charts, and do their business. Sometimes less is more, and the extra hardware of a fully customized sales office does not guarantee that you will make a profit.

Myth #18. You Can Earn a Living with Little Capital

Day Trading costs money. Trust me, I tried this trail, and the boy fell flat on his face.

Myth #19. You Should Only Sell Short

The market goes up and goes down. Why be worked-up with one or the other? You should be flexible in your trading styles so that you can follow the main trend; however, you want.

Myth #20. Reading Books Is a Waste of Time

Although it is not possible to use the strategies provided in a daily trade book, the thought process could trigger creative thoughts, which can affect profits.

Myth #21. Moving Averages Are Worth Nothing

A moving average is one of the best ways to assess the strength of the main trend and whether you need to enter or exit a trade. You'll be amazed at how much the first is in moving averages.

Myth #22. You Have to Understand Elliott Wave to Earn Money

I'm not going to hit Elliott Wave, because it's too easy. Don't worry if you can't exactly assign wave three extensions to the primary wave. Do you understand everything?

Myth #23. Day Trading Penny-Stocks Is Easy

You better know what you are doing. You are focusing better on volatile stocks and not just on the fact that stocks are cheap. Things are often cheap for a reason.

Myth #24. Day Trading Options Are the Way to Go

I understand that you want to create this or that on horseback to eliminate your risk. Well, let me help you here, you can't avoid the risk. Trade shares directly; don't try to become an M.I.T assistant overnight. Leave the complicated Black grids to the experts.

Myth #25. Who Needs the Business Rules of the Day?

You do! If you go out without rules, the market will take your money. Imagine watching a soccer or football game without rules. All you would see is the chaos that will eventually lead two teams to face off on the field. Day trading is very similar. Borderless, it's only a matter of time before your account explodes.

Myth #26. Day Trading Algorithms

Stop wasting time writing the next excellent program that will print money from the market. The market is a living and breathing entity. If you think it is as simple as writing buy, sell, and stop orders, then my friend, unfortunately, you're wrong. Let the super-smart think tanks with hotlines to trade do their thing. Do not try to play in this pond; you don't have the resources, the experience, or the time to stress your model continually. Start taking responsibility for your trades and stop trusting the code. You can't code the logic of why birds come together, and you can't code the market; the variables are too infinite.

Myth #27. You Need an Advanced Degree for Day Trading

Trading is one of the last remaining meritocracies in the world. It does not matter your race, religion, level of education, or financial background. If you work hard and learn what it marks you, the sky is over. Traders with a lot of formal education often get the worst because they are used to being always right and cannot ignore the need to win every trade.

Myth #28. Day Trading Plans Are Boring

You don't want to make money, so don't write your business plan. How much do you plan to do per month? These are questions that most day traders do not ask because they never intend to withdraw money from the market. Day trading is considered by many traders to be a hobby. They are looking for action and don't mind making money.

Chapter 12. Average Income of a Day Trader

You can go to a reliable gauge of what an informal investor can make dependent on their area, beginning capital, and business status. Let's face it, a significant number of are thinking about going out without anyone else and are not hoping to find a new line of work.

Anybody that discloses to you a conclusive range for a day exchanging pay is likely pulling your leg. I may as was well be conversing with one of my children about Yo Gabba (it was one of their preferred shows on Nickelodeon).

The reason being, there is a large group of outside variables that play into how a lot of cash you can make. In this article, we will tear through all the lighten on the web and get down to cold hard certainties. Sit back, unwind, and get some espresso.

A Decision You Should Not Take Lightly

You ought not to trifle with this choice, and you should gauge the upsides and downsides. First of all, exchanging for another person will permit you the chance to use the devices and systems of an outfit that is ideally beneficial. A portion of the positives exchanging for another person is evacuating the weights of distinguishing both a triumphant framework and a tutor that can help you en route.

It is On the off chance that you are not beneficial "enough," be set up to have a more significant number of rules tossed at you than when you were in sixth grade. This degree of administration over your exchanging action is because of the reality you are utilizing another person's cash, so profit or become acclimated to somebody revealing to you how to relax.

The one significant upside for day exchanging for another person is you will get pay. This pay is likely insufficient to live on; however, you do get a check. At the point when you go out alone, there is no pay. You are a financial specialist wanting to make payments. We will go into this theme a lot further. Later on, however, I needed to ensure I express this forthright.

Licenses

On the slim chance that you choose to work for the firm and are exchanging customer's cash or conceivably interfacing with clients, you will require your Series 7 and perhaps your Series 63 permit.

Arrangement 7

The Series 7 will give you the permit to exchange. Last I checked, the test cost $305 and relying upon the outfit will be secured by the firm.

Arrangement 63

The Series 63 is the following test you should take after the Series 7. This test licenses you to request orders for stock inside a point of view state. A straightforward perspective about this is the 7 gives you the privilege to exchange on a government level, and the 63 enable you to work inside the limits of state laws.

I don't anticipate covering the theme of day exchanging for somebody finally because I haven't lived it. From what I do know, you are required to finish some in-house preparing programs for the firm you speak to. For venture houses, you will get a not too bad base pay, enough to keep you at the lower white-collar class extend for New York.

Know the Best Part

Your base stock merchant pay could go from 50,000 - 70,000 dollars the US, which is only enough for you to take care of your link tab, feed yourself and perhaps take a taxi or two. In any case, this not the slightest bit covers meals, vehicles, excursions, tuition-based schools, and so on.

In this way, I surmise you can rapidly observe that for you to be fruitful, you're going to need to make your reward. There is only one catch; you need to profit day exchanging. Superficially, this sounds sensible because you bring down your hazard profile by having another pay stream of a base compensation; in any case, you need to perform to remain utilized, and will just get around 10-30%% of the benefits you get from your exchanging movement.

In light of these numbers, you would need to make about 300k in exchanging benefits to break a 100k in compensation. Most likely about it, the advantage of exchanging with an organization is, after some time, your purchasing influence will increment, and you have none of the drawbacks dangers since it's the organization's cash. The key is ensuring you have a lot of money under administration.

As should be evident in the infographic over, the way to making genuine cash is to begin dealing with different assets.

You, in one way or another, draw that off, and you will make by and large 576k per year. Indeed you read that right.

I realize the 576k looks engaging; however, recall it is out and out hard labor to get to the highest point of the mountain. The other brings up to get out from the infographic is that the usual reward is beginning to drift higher and if things go as conjecture will surpass the downturn top not long from now. Along these lines, on the off possibility that one of your objectives is to profit, you are looking in the right business.

Regular Income Trading for a Company

The widely appealing individual can hope to make somewhere in the range of 100k and 175k. In conclusion, it is on the off chance that you are beneath normal, hope to get a pink slip.

In any case, pause - there's additional. Certainty, if we broaden our exploration past New York, you will see the regular pay for a "Merchant" is $89,496.

Open Trading Firms

Be that as it may, I can consider many employments where you can make near $89k, and it doesn't require the degree of responsibility and hazard taking required for exchanging. You might be thinking, "This person just revealed to me it could go as high as $250k to $500k in case I'm better than expected, where $89k becomes an integral factor."

What I have talked about so far are the pay rates for traded on an open market organization—good karma attempting to get precise information for the first-class universe of private value brokers. What you will discover are regularly the top brokers from the Chase and Bank of America's endeavor out to flexible investments, as a result of the opportunity in their exchanging choices and the more significant compensation potential.

Here's the most significant part, with the general population firms, corporate objectives will frequently drive a segment of your other targets. The magnificence of the multifaceted investment world is while there are still organization objectives, you have the chance to eat a more significant amount of what you slaughter.

It's nothing for a top broker to out-acquire their chief on the off chance that they carry enough an incentive to the firm. What amount do you figure you could make?

Advantages of day exchanging for an organization:

- Pay

- Medical advantages

- The renown of working for a venture bank or fence investments

- No danger of individual capital

- Climb the corporate positions to deal with various assets

- A drawback of day exchanging for an organization

- Must connect with customers

- Office legislative issues

- By and large, you get 20% of benefits (Public Firm)

Day Trading for a Prop Firm

Day exchanging for prop firms can feel similar to living on the edge. Like exchanging for an organization, you will get some preparation before the prop firm enables you to trade with their cash and approach their frameworks. From that point forward, all likenesses between exchanging for a prop firm and an organization contrast. Try not to expect any human services of paid downtime. You won't have a base compensation or yearly audits. The prop firms will expect you to store cash to begin utilizing their foundation.

The advantages are the prop firm will part benefits with you anyplace from a third and up to half. The drawbacks are again no compensation, and you bear a portion of the torment with regards to misfortunes. However, here's the rub, the explanation prop firm merchants make not precisely those for the speculation houses is access to capital. Since you are likely exchanging the exclusive firm proprietor's cash, the pool of assets you approach is constrained.

I would state a better than an expected broker for a prop firm can make about 150k to 250k every year. The typical broker will do somewhere in the range of 60k and 100k, and underperformers will have such huge numbers of position limits set for them, they are fundamentally rehearsing and not profiting. These underperformers will probably expel themselves from the game because rehearsing doesn't take care of the tabs.

Advantages:

- Split benefits with Prop Firm

- Low commission rates

- No Boss

- Increment Margin

- Utilize your cash-flow to begin

- Loss of individual riches

- Constrained preparing

- No medical advantages or paid downtime

- No vocation movement

- Just cause cash off what you to acquire

Day Trading Salaries State by State in the US

Notwithstanding the information showed in the infographic from the Office of the New York State Comptroller, I needed to make it a stride further to distinguish the beginning pay for a passage level exchanging work the country over. I arrived on a passage level to give a counter to the middle national normal of $89k for an exchanging work. Keep in mind that $89k is a normal of junior exchanging employments - right to the most senior.

Along these lines, in the situation that you are genuinely beginning and are offered $50k, you don't get disheartened.

We, as a whole, need to start someplace! True to form, the New England and Pacific districts of the nation have the most significant pay. Presently, these can be just ascribed to the standard average cost for essential items. However, you can discover your state to perceive what you can hope to make as a lesser dealer.

The Myth

A large number of the online articles are explicit about the benefit proportion you can expect when you become an informal investor. For instance, an article by Cory Mitchell that shows up on the Vantage Point Trading site spreads it out in detail and expects to start exchanging capital of $30,000:

"Accept your normal five exchanges for every day, so if you have 20 exchanging days a month, you make 100 exchanges for every month. You make $3,750; however, despite everything, you have commissions and perhaps some different charges. Your expense per exchange is $5/contract (full circle). Your bonus costs are: 100 exchanges x $5 x 2 agreements = $1000."

In Mitchell's model, your net after bonuses is $2,750. Since you began with $30,000 that is a month to month return of a little more than 9 percent, if you reinvest those benefits on a month to month premise, toward the finish of one year, you'll have an interest of $55,944 and change. Not awful, and the best news is, you don't have to get dressed for work.

Chapter 13. Money Management

What is Money Management?

Money management is not a new aspect of the financial management world. It started when there was a rise of capitalism. When the economy was under a system that was dominated by private owners, they had their private properties and gained on the profits. Money Management started in around 1600, and individuals only survive by depending on how effectively they get their income. In the present age, to be successful financially involves having the ability and the zeal to save more, and lean on investing any surplus.

Money management is a term to refer to the many ways people manage their financial resources. It ranges from budget planning in regards to their income. Money management involves planning and purchasing items that are important to you. Without planning well and lack of money management skills, the amount a person has will always not be enough for them.

Before anyone starts on the money management journey, you need to be aware of the assets and liabilities that you have. Some of the examples of Personal assets and properties are cars, home, retirement, investment, and bank accounts. On the other hand, personal liabilities are loans, debts, and mortgages. To be able to know your net worth, you should see the difference between your assets and liabilities. When the liabilities are higher than the assets, then you have a lower net worth. Having excellent money management skills, you will be able to avoid this.

Goal setting helps in Money management. Without goal setting, you will be worried about daily bill management; this can adversely affect your long term goals. With goal setting, you can have a clear view of the expenses needed to, and which needs to be cut out. A perfect example is when you have a goal of getting a car worth $30,000; your goals will be to cut down your expenses. Similar to someone whose goals are to get a $20,000 car?

After planning and knowing your goals, start creating your budget. A budget is an estimation of income for a defined time — a tool that will assist you in managing your money well. With a budget, you will be able to save some cash and be able to minimize impulse buying. An example of a reasonable budget will be to allocate $250 for entertainment and miscellaneous expenses a month after settling the basic needs. If your income increases, it would be advisable to add the extra income to your savings plan and not adding it to the expenses budget.

When budgeting, you will have multiple accounts to manage. For example, you may have an emergency fund and saving accounts. By doing this, you will avoid the temptations of spending the funds on impulse buying. The retirement plan should be kept separate from the other accounts. There are different software that you can use to assist you in money management. An example of money management software is Quicken; it helps in tracking your various accounts and ensuring your saving and spending goals are on the right track.

The different aspects of money management include analyzing, planning, and executing a financial portfolio. The financial portfolio includes investment types, taxes, savings, and banking. In business management, there are economic variables that might affect your business finances. The best

Money Management skills are to be able to access and control all the factors that might affect your financial position.

You can achieve your set goals through excellent money management. A dream of owning a home without using student loans, and be able to have a stress-free life from debts. Have a better plan to be able to deal with unpredictable events that can affect your finances, like loss of employment, serious illness. With Money Management, you will be able to have some savings that will cover your unexpected events.

The Internet is a global computer network that contains information and provides communication. Banking, investment, and insurance needs did not exist before. In the past days, customers had restrictions on decisions making in their financial matters, with less information on their options in their local areas. With the lack of internet connection, there was limitation and restrictions on where to find the right information. People had to go shopping for different items, like furniture and electronics. And also the purchasing of mortgages and insurance policies.

Money Management Skills

Do you know your income expenditure? Do you know your shopping, clothing and entertainment expenses? Money Management is a life skill that is not in the school curriculum. Most people learn it from our parents on how to handle money. Since most people didn't learn about financial skills in school, you can still learn them now. Here are some of the Money management skills that you can follow to improve your skills.

Set a Budget

Track how you spend your money. Do you spend on food, movies, entertainment, and clothes? Do you frequently have an overdraw of your bank account? If this is true, then set a budget. Check your bank statements and note down how much your expenditure is categorical. You will find out how much wastage of money you are not aware of.

Spend Wisely

Have a shopping list when you go to the grocery store? Do you first check the price of an item before putting the item in your basket? Use coupons if available. Use online resources and mobile apps to stay focused on your expenditure.

Monitor your spending! By not being attentive to these small tips, you will keep on losing money. It takes time to get coupons, and it takes some effort to find coupons and writing a shopping list and checking the price of an item before buying. It will all be worth it in the long run.

Balance Your Books

Most people rely on going online to look at their bank balance. By doing this, you won't be able to know how much you are spending at the moment. The best advice is to be accountable by recording all your expenses; you will have avoided over-spending.

Set a Plan

You must have a plan for you to accomplish anything. For you to go from location A to B, it won't be possible without a GPS to show the routes. You will end up driving aimlessly going nowhere. This is similar to not having a financial plan. You will always be broke and not knowing where your money is spent on. "Where did that money go?" With a great plan, you will be able to track your money and expenditure.

Think Like an Investor

The education system does not teach about handling money, mainly how to invest in growing your wealth. The rich people did not just save $500 a month; they learned how to grow their savings and invest. Turning that $500 into $1000, then into $10,000 and eventually into $100,000 and more. By investing and growing your money, you will have secured a stable financial future. Think like an investor, and see your money grow.

Have the Same Financial Goals with Your Partner/Spouse

If you're married and you have a joint bank account, then learn to work together. You must both agree with the financial goals. Make a budget and also see a financial adviser to learn how to invest your money. You must ensure that you have the same financial goals and stay focused.

Save Money

Have a strong commitment to saving your money and securing your future. You can improve your financial situation and make it better! But you need to start with the decision to do so. Decide to start saving your money and improving your management skills.

Importance of Money Management

Look for great price bargains and avoiding bad deals when purchasing. When you start earning more money, understanding how to invest will become an essential way of reaching your goals like having down payment for a home.

Understanding the importance of excellent money management will help you achieve your plans and future goals. Some of the importance of Money Management is going to be discussed below.

Better Financial Security

Being cautious of your expenditures and saving, you will be able to save enough for the future. Saving will give you financial security to deal with any unexpected expenses or emergencies like loss of employment, your car breaking down, or even saving for a holiday. Having savings, you will not have to use a Credit card to settle crises. Saving is a crucial part of money employment as it helps you build your financial security for a secured future.

Take Advantage of Opportunities

You may encounter opportunities to invest in a business to make more money or an exciting experience like a good deal on a holiday vacation. A friend may inform you of a great investment opportunity or get a tremendous once-in-a-lifetime dream holiday vacation. It can be frustrating not having the money to jump right to these opportunities.

Pay Lower Interest Rates

With excellent money management skills, you can determine your credit score. The highest score means you pay your bills on time and with low-level total debt.

Having a higher credit score, you can save more of what you have and have a lower interest rate for car loans, mortgages, credit cards, and even car insurance. And there is the chance to brag to your friends about your high credit score at the parties.

Reduce Stress and Conflict

Paying your bills on time can have a relieving feeling. But on the other hand, being late in paying your bills cause stress and have a negative impact like shutdown in your gas and water supply. Always being broke before your next paycheck can bring conflict and a significant amount of stress for, couple. And, as we all know, stress brings health problems, experts say, like hypertension, insomnia, and migraines. Being aware of how you can manage your finances, so you have extra cash and savings can put your mind at ease. You will enjoy a stress-free life.

Earn More Money

With your income growing, your financial planning will not only include budgeting for monthly expenses but also figuring out where to invest the extra cash that has accumulated. Knowing different kinds of investments, for example, stocks and mutual funds, you can earn more money from the investments than what you could have made by leaving the money in your savings account in your bank. But be aware not all investments are recognized as a good investment idea, for example, offshore casinos. One of the best benefits of having investments, you can be at work earning monthly income, and your investments, on the other hand, are making more money for you.

More Saving and Time

Excellent money management can assist in avoiding your finances from spiraling out of control. It is easy to be in debt if you are unaware of how all your income it's spent monthly. Effective money management means better use of your spare time. You can spend time with your family and friends by having a clear budget; you will be able to plan for fun days out as you will have available cash to do so.

Chapter 14. Creating Your Own Day Trading Strategy

As you start to get more into day trading, you may decide to develop your strategy. There are a lot of great trading strategies that are out there, but there may be some market conditions or other situations where you need to be able to develop your strategy. Or, after trying out a few different things, you end up finding a new strategy, or a combination of strategies, that ends up working out the best.

Over time, you must find your place inside the market. As you go through, you may even find that you would rather be more like a swing trader rather than a day trader just because of the different available methods.

The good news is, there is a market for any kind of trader, and there are a million types of strategies that you can use based on your personal preferences along the way.

Before you jump into the market as a beginner with your trading strategy, you must start by picking one of the strategies (or another proven strategy that you have researched). You need to have some time to try out a strategy and tread through the market a bit before you start coming up with your strategy. Even if you have invested in the stock market before, you will find that working with day trading is entirely different compared to some of the other methods available, and you do not want to pick a strategy that may have worked with one of your other trades. Still, you will make you fail miserably with day trading.

It is all about spending some time in the market and getting familiar with the market. You will want to get familiar with how the day trading market works, how to recognize good stocks, and so on before you make a good strategy that can help you. After spending some time in the market, working with one or two strategies that you like, you will be able to learn the patterns that you like and what to watch out for, and it becomes so much easier to make a strategy that will actually work.

But no matter where you are as a trader, it is so essential that every trader has a strategy of some sort to help them get started. It is so easy for beginners just to pick out stock and then start trading without having a plan in place at all. This is a dangerous thing to work with. It pretty much leaves the decisions up to your emotions, and we all know how dangerous this can be when you are first starting out. You should never leave your trades up to the emotions; this will make you stay in the market too long or leave the market too early, and you will end up losing money.

Learn all of the rules that go with that strategy, how to make that strategy work for you, and exactly how you should behave at different times in the market with that strategy. Even if it ends up leading you to a bad trade (remember that any type of strategy and even the best traders will end up with a bad trade on occasion), you will stick it out until the trade is made.

You can always switch strategies in between trades, but it is never a good idea to switch your strategy once you are already in the market.

Switching strategies can seem tempting when you are a beginner in the market. You may see that things are going south or may realize once you are in the market that you should have done a different strategy from the beginning. But as you look through some of the strategies, you probably notice that they are a bit different, and they need some different requirements before you can get in and out of the trade. Switching in the middle is not going to work and will lead to an automatic loss.

The most important thing that you can remember when you become a day trader is that all traders will fail at some point. Many beginners will fail because they do not take the time to learn how to properly day trade, or they let their emotions get in the way of making smart decisions. But even advanced traders will have times when they will fail and lose money as well.

The market is not always the most reliable thing in the world. Even when you are used to reading the charts and looking at the market, there will be times when it does not act as expected, and a trader will lose out. Or the advanced trader may choose to try out a new strategy, and it does not work that well for them.

This is also why you need to consider how much you can afford to lose on a trade before you enter the market. You do not want to go all out on your first trade because it is likely you will fail and lose that money or maybe more depending on the trade.

If you are worried about getting started in the market or you want to mess around and try out a few of the strategies ahead of time to see how they work, especially if you are using one of your strategies, then you should consider working with a simulator. Sometimes you will be able to get one of these from your broker to try out and experiment with the market, and sometimes you may have to pay a bit from another site to use this simulator. However, this can be a valuable tool that will help you to try out different things, make changes, and get a little familiarity in the market before you invest your actual money. As a beginner, if you have access to one of these simulators, it is worth your time to give it a try.

Picking Your Trade Based on the Time of Day

Before we move on, we will take a look at which types of strategies seem to work the best at different times of the day. As you get into the market, you will notice that each period of the day will be different, and some patterns seem to show up over time with them. We will work with three times of day, the open, the mid-day, and the close. If you want to be successful with day trading, it is not a good idea to use the same strategy at all three times of the day because these strategies will not be successful at all times of the day.

The best traders will figure out what time of day they get the most profitable trades, and then they will make some adjustments to their strategies and their trading to fit them into these profitable times.

First, let's talk about the open. This period will last about an hour and a half, starting at 9:30 in the morning on New York Times. It is a busy time of the day because people are joining the market for the first time, or they are making adjustments based on how their stocks had done overnight. Because this time is so busy, it can also be a profitable period if you play the game right.

The best strategies to use during the open will be the VWAP trades and the Bull Flag Momentum.

The next session is the mid-day session, and this will start at 11 in the morning and go for about four hours. This is a slow time in the market, and it is considered one of the more dangerous times to trade during the day. There is not going to be much liquidity or volume in the market. Even a smaller order will make a stock move quite a bit during this time, so you need to watch the market if you are holding onto your stocks. It is more likely that you will be stopped with unexpected and strange moves during this period.

It is common for many traders, both beginners and those who are more advanced, to have a lot of trouble during the mid-day. Many decide that it is not the best idea to work in the market during this time. But if you do decide to trade, it is essential to keep the stops tight and also to lower your share size. You should also be picky about the risk and reward ratio during this time. You will find that new traders will often do their overtrading during this time, and it may be best to avoid trading during this period altogether simply.

If you do decide to trade during the mid-day, it is best to watch the stocks as closely as possible, get some things ready for a close, and always be very careful about any trading decisions that you try to do. You will find that support or resistance trades, moving average, VWAP, and reversal strategies work well during the mid-day.

And finally, there is the close, which starts at 3 in the afternoon and goes for about an hour. These stocks are considered more directional, so it is best to stick with those that are going either down or up during this last hour. It is possible to raise the tier size compared to what it was at in mid-day, but you do not want to go as high as you were at open. You will find that the prices at closing are often going to reflect what the traders on Wall Street think the value of the stocks is.

These traders have stayed out of the market during the day, but they have been closely watching things so that they can get in and dominate what happens during the last little bit of trading.

It is also common to see that many market professionals will sell their stocks at this time and take the profits because they do not want to hold onto the trades overnight. As a day trader, you will be one of these professionals because you need to sell all of your stocks on the same day to be a day trader.

If you notice that the stock starts to move higher during this last hour, this means that the professionals are considered bullish on that stock. However, if you see that the stock starts to move lower in that last hour, it means that the professionals in the market are considered bearish. It is best during this last hour to work with trades that go with these professionals, rather than making trades that go against them.

When you decide to trade in the closing hour, you will want to use the moving average trades, support and resistance trades, or VWAP to get the best results.

Chapter 15. The Basics Of Options

For you to succeed, you need the basic knowledge of what you want to do, for it will help you on how to do things the right way with less trouble. To fit in the options trading game, you need to know the basic knowledge about this type of trading to be on the safer side. We shall take a look at the strategies you can use, the types of options, how it works, and its drawbacks.

Strategies Used in Options Trading

Strategies are the set of guidelines you need to follow to achieve amazing results in what you are doing, and options trading has its strategies, too. Let us now dig deeper into a number of the strategies that you need to implement.

Covered Call Strategy

It is a market transaction where an individual, mostly an investor who is offering call options for sale, owns the same size as the market trade. It is executed when the individual with the long term asset writes the call options on the asset. Covered call strategy is a popular strategy because of its capability to minimize risks and promote income generation.

It is mostly applied when you, as an investor, have an asset with a short term and short position, wanting to hold it for long for you to receive the options premiums. A seller who has fantastic knowledge of covered call strategy gets higher profits as compared to other strategies. The drawback of this strategy is that an individual does not receive full options premium when the stock rises above the strike price.

Long Straddle Strategy

This is an options strategy where a trader purchases an asset that has both the extended standard options and put-call. Also, the agreed price plus the time of expiry usually are similar. This strategy generates massive profits by having long put and calls options. The long call practice in the market happens when long put expires, and there is a rise in the price of the instrument. Moreover, the long put is practiced only in the fall of the stock's price scenario. You are advised to use this strategy when you think the volatility of the stock will be significant through the trade term. You suffer losses if your underlying stock comes in between the upper and lower breakeven point.

Short Straddle Strategy

It is a risky strategy that is the vice versa of the long straddle options strategy. As an investor, you are advised to apply this strategy when there are chances of low volatility in the market. You are likely to suffer from significant losses when the stock behaves significantly in the market. The investor generates income and holds on the premium when the stock behavior in the market does not have much change in either direction.

Long Strangle Strategy

How does long strangle strategy work? Here is the answer to it. An investor purchases typically out of money standard options and puts calls simultaneously on the instrument with a similar time of expiry. Out of the money call option is a call option with a lower market price than the price agreed on an asset. Conversely, out of the money put option is a market situation in the case that an asset has a price above the strike price.

Most of the investors who apply this strategy have the belief that the asset will have a massive change in its behavior but are not sure in which direction. It is a cheaper strategy with limited losses compared to straddle because of the options which are purchased out of the money.

Iron Butterfly Strategy

Iron butterfly strategy involves selling and purchasing an at the money put and also at the money call. All of the options usually have the same expiration dates on the asset. It is named after a creature because the short put and call are offered for sale at the middle strike price forming the body part of a butterfly, while the wings come into formation when the put and call options are purchased either above or below the middle strike price.

Most traders use this strategy when they believe there will be no changes in the stock's price within the time of expiry. You have a higher likelihood of getting huge profits when you are near the strike price in the middle.

Iron Condor Strategy

It is an options strategy that involves the sale of out of the money call and put spread on a similar instrument (preferably asset) with a similar date of expiration. It is created when the trader offers the out of the money put for sale and purchases another one of a lower strike price. Also, created by offering one out of the money call for sale and purchases another one of a higher strike price. The call and put spreads are generally of the same width. Many traders prefer this strategy because of the capability of generating massive credit on the same risk as compared to other options strategies.

Long call butterfly spread. In this type of strategy, a trader normally utilizes both bull and bear call spread strategies with three different strike prices on similar instruments and time of expiry. A trader purchases typically two contracts for options where one is of a greater agreed price than the other contract. Also, there is a sale of two other contract options at a price in the middle. The price agreed should be equivalent to the amount you get when you distinguish the top strike price and the lowest one.

Protective Collar Strategy

This strategy is exercised when you purchase a put and conversely write a call with the situation of out of the money in the market. It takes place on a similar stock with a similar time of expiry. Combining long put and the short call forms the collar of the stock, which is usually established by the agreed prices of the options. Its protective feature, moreover, comes up from the capability of the put option to offer protection on the stock until on the expiration of the option. Bear put spread trading strategy.

A trader on this strategy buys put options at an agreed price then offers a similar amount of put for sale at a lower price. A similar type of option is on the same stock with the same date of expiration. Most bearish traders use this strategy with the expectations that the price of the stock will drop. The advantage of this strategy is its ability to offer minimal losses though it also offers minimal profits, which is a turn off for most traders.

Bull Calls Strategy

You, as an investor, purchase calls at an agreed price and simultaneously offer the calls for sale at a greater agreed price. Happens typically in similar instruments having a similar time of expiration. Most bullish traders use this strategy expecting there will be an average increase in the price of the stock to gain profits.

Long Put Trading Strategy

It is a bearish options trading strategy. An investor who uses this strategy expects the stock will move become lower before the time of expiration. Risks involved here are minimal to the amount of premium paid. Short put trading strategy. Unlike the long put options strategy, a short put strategy is utilized mostly when the trader is bullish about the stock, that is, expects a rise in the stock's price. In any case, the agreed price becomes lower than that of the asset; then, the trader makes massive profits. The losses incurred here are unlimited.

Why Use Options?

- You only need minimum initial cash outlay to purchase options as compared when buying stock in trading.

- Options such as call options enable investors to enter the market at a cheaper cost.

- Options also help investors to generate more income. It is seen mostly by using the covered call options trading strategy. The investor holds on to the stock believing the price will have few changes. As in, either to remain stable or increase a little.

- Purchasing calls and put options enable traders to invest with minimal risks since the major thing they can lose is premium.

- Using options will offer you more investment alternatives since it is a flexible trading tool.

How Options Work

After knowing the strategies and the reasons why to use options, let us now know how this type of trading works. Below are some of the details I have for you:

- Options have a time frame. They always have their date of expiration. You should be able to know their time frame to make profits. After they expire, you do not have the right to purchase or offer stock for sale at a specified price. The shorter the time it has till expiry, the lower the value of the option.

- Options have different strike prices, which generally indicate the price of the stock.

- Options offer you the right to purchase or offer stock for sale.

- Purchasing an option gives you the honor to purchase or offer the stock for sale.

- Selling an option gives you the honor of delivering the stock at an agreed price. The stock's current price is not under consideration.

Chapter 16. Why Invest in Swing Trading?

How to Make Profits from Swing Trading

To understand how you can profit from swing trading, it can be helpful to look at a couple of mock-up charts. Asset prices fluctuate down all the time and on different time scales. In its most straightforward form, swing trading takes advantage of the swings up and down on the markets – you buy low and sell high.

Of course, any investor can say they hope to buy low and sell high. The swing trader hopes to capitalize on a swing or a single move in the asset price. Swing traders hope to earn profits from breakouts when the asset price increases to a new level. Alternatively, you can short the asset if its experiencing a major decline. Swing traders can also earn smaller profits as the asset price bounces higher and lower about the median.

This graphic indicates price levels of support and resistance for some financial assets. Our goal in this chart is to look for an opportunity to buy the asset when the price is low, and then sell it when the price rises. There are many techniques a trader will use to estimate the right times to enter a position.

It is a price level that historical data have shown that as the price of the asset decreases, it will stop and reverse and enter into an increasing trend after it reaches the support point. So an asset that is trading at the support pricing level is one that a trader wants to invest in – if there are signals of an uptrend. There are other opportunities to get in on trade as well at higher pricing levels. A trader will enter a position if there are signals that the asset price will continue increasing to the resistance level. So, we say that a swing trader will buy at support. This is if you expect the asset price to increase. If you expect it to decrease, then you sell at resistance.

To make a profit, the trader needs to know when to exit a trade. The resistance level provides the best opportunity to do so. Profiting from your trades can take discipline, there is always a chance that the asset will break above the resistance level, and emotions make people anxious to take advantage of such situations. But waiting too long to exit a position can be costly if the price drops rapidly back to the support level. It's important to understand that swing trading is not gambling. The trader uses technical analysis to determine the best prices at which to buy and sell to profit from the trade. But the concept is pretty simple for increasing prices – identify levels of support and resistance and buy low when pricing is at or near the support level, and there are indications of an upward trend. Then you sell high at a pricing point that you determine to make profits and exit the trade.

The many tools of technical analysis can give you a solid indication of coming price trends, and the mood of the markets. But it's important to be realistic and recognize that no tool is foolproof, and you can't win on every trade. The bottom line is the indicators aren't right 100% of the time. Swing traders can also earn profits from declining asset prices. For example, you can short stocks or purchase put options. If you don't understand how that works now, don't worry, we will talk about that in the following pages.

For now, let's just understand the overall picture. This time you enter your position when the asset price is relatively high and all the signals are pointing to a coming downward trend. Then when the price drops to a practical level, you exit the position. Graphically it looks like this. It is the central idea behind swing trading. Of course, in practice, it's not that simple; otherwise, everyone would be doing it and raking in millions of dollars. Becoming a successful and profitable swing trader requires mastering the tools of technical, chart, and fundamental analysis so that you know when to enter and exit positions, and whether to go long or short your positions. For now, let's take a step back and take a look at the three biggest markets where swing trading is used.

Swing Trading with Forex

Forex is the foreign exchange market where the various currencies of the world are traded against one another. Forex isn't just in the United States, there are trading markets around the globe, so it's a huge market, with $5 trillion traded daily – compared to $200 billion on the stock market. The largest markets are in New York, London, Tokyo, and Singapore. Currencies around the world are traded in pairs, so you could trade the dollar against the Great British Pound, or the Dollar against the Yen, or the Euro against the Pound, for example. While all currencies in the world are traded, the focus is mostly on currencies used in the largest economies, including the Euro, the British Pound, the US Dollar, and the Japanese Yen.

Unlike the stock market, which goes through brokerages that charge high commissions, Forex is traded over the counter with small or no commissions. Since there are markets worldwide, it's open 24 hours a day, 5-days a week. It's also highly liquid. That means there is enough volume in trading activity to enter and exit positions quickly, making it well suited for swing trading. During any business day of the week, traders can open and close positions 24 hours a day. It's also possible for traders to utilize a great deal of leverage on the Forex markets as well.

Swing trading on Forex doesn't require a huge time commitment. You can check your charts a couple of times a day, so it is suitable for someone with other things going on in their life like a job, which makes it hard for them to sit at the computer all day long. Several swing trading methods are used on the Forex markets, including candlestick trading, trend trading, range trading, mean reversion trading, chart analysis, and Bollinger band trading.

Swing Trading with Options

You can think of it as an old-style hourglass, with the sand in the upper part of the hourglass representing the time value of the option. As it drains into the bottom part of the glass, the option is losing value, and eventually, the time value all drains away. However, if the strike price is lower than the market price, the option still has value and can even be exercised, which means that the buyer of the option can elect actually to buy the shares. Because of that intrinsic value, call options gain value with the rising stock price.

Options also make it easy to profit from downturns in stock price. In this case, you would purchase a put option, which gives the buyer the option to sell a stock to the writer. Of course, put options also come with an expiration date, so the decreasing time value also impacts the pricing of put options. Options are inherently short term assets, making them ideal for swing trading. The shortest term for an option is one week, so that the option will expire a week after its issued. Most options are monthly, but there are longer-term options that can expire up to one or two years from the current date. Those are called LEAPS, which means Long Term Equity Anticipation Security.

Options can be purchased on many securities, as well as on indexes. They represent a great opportunity for swing traders because they don't require much capital to invest upfront, and some strategies can be used to limit risk. For swing traders, the same tools and analysis that would be used with stocks are used with options, since the value of the option is directly related to the changing price of the underlying stock. However, the swing trader of options needs to pay attention to the expiration dates of any options in their portfolio. Swing traders who trade options will primarily use the techniques that swing traders of stocks will use.

Swing Trading Stocks

Swing trading stocks are top-rated since there are many highly volatile stocks, and stocks tend to breakout to the upside or downside quite often. While the stock market is less liquid than Forex, because of the way the markets behave, stocks can be more amenable to many swing trading strategies. A swing trader on the stock market can profit from price appreciation by going long and can also shorten their positions when appropriate.

Swing traders on the stock market will utilize all the strategies of swing trading. This will include trading with the trend, looking for breakouts, Bollinger band trading, chart pattern analysis, candlestick trading, and more. Swing trading has some similarities to other styles of trading and investing, but there are also many differences. Swing trading is not something that a Warren Buffett style investor would be interested in.

Chapter 17. Working with a Technical Analysis

The first strategy that we are going to look at is known as technical analysis. We will go into more detail about this one, but pretty much any strategy that will rely on charts and graphs to help you make a decision is going to be considered a technical analysis.

Technical analysis is a strategy that is going to be used to help us evaluate investments and identify some of the different forms of trading opportunities by looking at all of the statistical trends that have been gathered up over time with the trading activity.

The trends that are sometimes studied here are going to include volume and price movement.

Unlike what we are often going to see when we work with fundamental analysis, this kind of analysis is going to look at a lot of charts and graphs to find the patterns of price movements, look at some of the trading signals that are out there, and even look at some of the other analytical charting tools to figure out the weakness or the strengths of security.

We can use this analysis on any security, though, that has historical trading data. It means this strategy works on currencies, fixed income, commodities, stocks, and futures, to name a few.

The Basics

The technical analysis is going to be a form of investing strategy that believes that the activity in the past for trading, and the past price changes of security, will be the best indicators to perform in the future. They can use this analysis along with fundamental analysis in some cases, but it is sometimes done just on its own.

This one is going to assume that the security is already priced right where it should be. With fundamental analysis, the investor believes that they can find a security that is discounted based on its perceived worth, lack of debts, equity, assets, and more. But technical analysis is going to assume that all of this is found in the price of your security already and that there is no such thing as an overpriced or discounted security at all.

There are going to be two main methods that are going to be used to help analyze securities and make some right investment decisions. These are technical analysis and fundamental analysis. Fundamental analysis is going to involve us going through some of the financial statements of a company to help determine the fair value of the business. On the other hand, though, technical analysis assumes that the price of a security is already going to reflect all of the information that is publicly available to the public and then will spend more time focusing on the price movements and analyzing these.

To keep it simple, the technical analysis is going to spend a lot of time trying to look more at the sentiment of the market behind the trends in the price by looking for trends and patterns and seeing how that may affect what is going on in the market. This is preferable to a lot of investors, especially with a day trader, rather than looking at some of the fundamental attributes that may be found with the security.

Assumptions of Technical Analysis

There are three main assumptions that we can focus on when it comes to using technical analysis. These are going to include some of the following. The market is already going to discount everything. The analysts who work with this one believe that everything, including the fundamentals of a company to market psychology, and even broad market factors, are already going to be put into the price of the stock.

This is important to them because it removes any of the need to consider the factors separately before we make an investment decision. The only thing that is going to remain for us to look through and analyze at this point is the price movements. In technical analysis, this is going to be viewed as the product of supply and demand for a particular stock in the market.

Price Is Going to Move in Trends

This is where we are going to need the charts and graphs because they can tell us so much about how the stock has performed in the past. And it is going to make a world of difference when it comes to helping us see where the price is going to head in the future. The more historical price movement we can get in charts and graphs, the better.

Technical analysts often believe that prices are going to move in trends. There are different trends based on the amount of time you want to focus on, but there will be some trends there. In other words, this is an idea that will bet on the stock price, continuing like it did in the past rather than move erratically.

History Will Repeat Itself

Another part here that a technical analyst is going to focus on is the idea that history will repeat itself. Despite what we may think, this is going to be predictable and is based on the emotions of those who go in the market, and whether they feel excitement or fear.

Technical analysis is going to use patterns in the chart in order to figure out more about these emotions and how they will change the movements in the market. This helps us to predict which direction a stock is likely to go, and we can make our purchases and sales based on that information.

How to Use a Technical Analysis

This is a strategy that is going to spend a good deal of time trying to forecast some of the price movements of pretty much any instrument that you would want to trade, as long as it is going to be, on the average, subject to the different forces of supply and demand. This means that you can work with a technical analysis of currency pairs, futures, bonds, and stocks.

Some view this kind of strategy as just a study of the supply and demand forces and that these are going to be shown as the price movements of the market on some of the graphs and charts that are used. You will find that this kind of analysis is going to most likely, apply to some of the price changes. Still, there are a few analysts of this nature who will track numbers in addition to the price, including the open interest figures and the trading volume.

Across the industry, there are going to be lots of signals and patterns that are developed by researchers to help us see the benefit of working with this kind of analysis and getting the best results I the process. These analysts have also come in and developed many systems of trading to help them forecast what is going to happen in the market and trade on those price movements.

Some indicators that we will want to use are more focused on figuring out the trend in the current market, including the resistance and the support areas. Then some are more focused on determining the strength of a new trend and how likely it is that this trend is going to continue along the way. Some of the technical indicators and charting patterns that we can use will include momentum indicators, moving averages, channels, and trendlines.

Technical analysts have also developed a lot of trading systems to make it easier to forecast and then trade on a price movement. Some of the indicators are going to be focused on identifying the trend in the market that is current. Commonly used indicators of technical analysis and some of the charting patterns include channels, trendlines, momentum indicators, and more. To keep this simple, technical analysis is going to look at the following indicators to help make things possible, including:

The support and resistance levels:

- Moving averages

- Oscillators

- Volume and momentum indicators

- Chart patterns

- Price trends

- The Limitations of a Technical Analysis

While there are a lot of different parts that come with technical analysis, there are also a few limitations that we are going to notice when it comes to working with technical analysis. The major hurdle that is going to come in is the legitimacy of the economic principle of the efficient market hypothesis. According to this, the market prices are going to reflect all of the past and current information already, so there is no way for us to take advantage of the patterns or the wrong prices to earn some more in profits.

Many fundamental analysts and economists are going to believe that inefficient markets will find that it is hard to believe that any actionable information is contained in the historical price and volume data and that history is not going to repeat them. Instead, they believe that prices are going to move more as something random.

A second criticism that comes up is that it works in some cases, but it is only going to work because of a self-fulfilling kind of prophecy. For example, a lot of the traders that use this are indeed going to place their stop-loss order below the 200-day moving average of a certain company. Because of this, you are then going to see some of the other traders look at the price decrease and choose to sell their positions to avoid losing money. This is going to reinforce the trend as well.

Even with some of these shortcomings, there are a lot of benefits to working with the technical analysis. There are a lot of traders, especially those who are working with day trading, who will work with this method because it is going to provide them with the results they need. And knowing the movements of the charts will often be enough to help them to see success with this kind of trading since it is shorter in length. But doing a combination of the fundamental analysis and the technical analysis has served a lot of traders in the process as well, so it depends on your trading style and what seems to work the best for you.

Chapter 18. Emotion vs. Performance

Containing your emotions and being disciplined walk hand in hand in maintaining successful trade. Having emotions is natural as a human, but these emotions, if not properly managed, can send your trade on a downhill path directs to failure, but that is not our desire. Our findings have been summarized to several guidelines on how you can have these emotions in line and how to use them to your advantage.

How to Control Your Emotions as a Trader

It is essential that as a trader, you should be at full capacity to control your emotions. Letting these weaknesses go out of hand will be fatal for your trade. It can easily ruin all the hard-earned profits in a night. An example is when you have experienced several losses in your trade; you end up over-leveraging, destroying your account with a single trade.

A well-equipped trader should know that trade is a game, and as a game, there are chances that you will lose one time and win the other nothing is static. You need to stay detached from the results of every trade and have an open mind. Having an emotional attachment on every trade will just inhibit growth as a trader as you will be in constant fear of repeating the same mistakes if you had losses. When you had profits, you might end up sticking onto that one trade idea, not taking note of the different trends in the market. Expect anything prepares for everything.

You need to focus when involving yourself in day trade. Focus on your goal; focus on your objectives. You need to know what to do to have your trade-in control. If you want to achieve all those goals and objectives, what can you actually do to have your emotions in control and work on not spoil your trade? These can be easily achieved if you just follow these simple guidelines:

One, you need to take a break; however, small it is and just walk it out or just listening to music. Knowing the rush nature of the day trade, you need a break lest you will be trapped in uncontrollable emotions. To have a break from the constant high tempo at which you are trading, you need to off yourself from your trade for a while. Doing this will help clear your mind and is also a reminder that you are the one in control. You control the trade, and the market doesn't push you to trade. You can also opt for meditating on your break as it will also prove to be very beneficial for you. Meditation will enable you to drain away any stressful thought, all the negative energy, and allow positive inner peace to dwell.

Check on volatility. When are the prices in the market volatile? You will work best when the prices are in this state. Working in a congested market will lead to frustrations, and we don't want that, do we? You first get frustrated; then you are angry after that you are fully stressed, and then pretty soon, your will waves of emotions clouding your judgment.

You need to have a break on trading after three losing or winning trades' follow-ups. After three wins, why will we advise you to stop, you are the super trader after all. Well, this is exactly why we are telling you to take a short break, how you view yourself. This self-pride will pretty much be the downfall of you and your trades, as you will end up overtrading and over leveraging. This can drastically pull you down. What if you have three follow up losses? The losses will put you down, and you have diminishing thoughts on yourself, making you feel like a loser making you. This overflow of emotions can easily affect your confidence as a trader and your judgment as you go by the trade.

Another guideline is that you should not be so focused on your previous profits or losses while in trade. Do not constantly be on these figures. If something is bound to make you emotional, in your trade, it is your profit and loss records. Many traders take this as a scale of your self-worth and value. This is the wrong perception to be having in mind when venturing into a trade.

Lastly, you need to ask yourself this vital question, do I fear? Traders are normal human beings, and as beings, they are prone to the feeling of fear, to be afraid, and to get scared. This is an intense emotion and so destructive, is it? If the answer is yes, that you do fear, you need to go back and review what rules are placed in trade, go through your strategies, and the plans you set. Ensure you have confidence that you have made the right choice, and then finally reduce the size of your trade to a size more appropriate, which you can easily handle.

These guidelines are few but have a lot of weight, follow these steps, and watch how you will rise. But always have it in mind that mastery of your emotions is important, but it does not give you a trading edge. This comes about with your trading methods.

Having to conquer and control our emotions is key, but you also need to work on your disciple. Having a trade disciple can take those emotions. Despite it being hard to master, we have simplified it for you as we have your best interest at heart. As a trader, you need to have established a routine for the premarket, and you should have productive training habits. You also need to have it in mind that trading disciple is practiced at all times.

Lack of discipline during trade will lead to making mistakes common in the trade, such as rushing into things without taking time to reflect on their outcomes. It might end up executing the trade prematurely, and you will also risk violating the management rules, you will get caught up in the act of over-trading and revenge trading. All this will have a final result, loss of money, and emotional trauma.

How to Be Disciplined in Your Trade

One, you need to lay down a trading plan. Take time and plan before you start your session. Analyze what instruments are in your possession, have trade scenarios that are specific to your trade, and take note of all ideas that will be advantageous to the trade. This prevents you from entering the trade prematurely and without knowledge of trade mistakes. You will also line your trade and the strategies you had planned out for it.

Secondly, you need to mind the trade routines. You always need to follow your trade routine. Set a trading routine consisting of your analysis of the premarket, the hours that major markets trade and the days end hours. Have a usual check of the economic trade calendar for any report and analyze the trade prizes. You should work on never breaking your routine. Let it be fixed and static.

You are required to review your trades and have a journal on your trade. Reviewing your trades will help you learn from that experience. What did you not do right, and how you could have done it better? What new techniques will better work this time around? Your former trades should be taken in as a learning experience and as a lift to the higher economic ground. They should not be used to put you down, but they are meant to elevate you even higher.

Have reminders of the trade. This may appear rather unprofessional, but it is advantageous in the long run. Keep reminders of the mistakes you made in the previous trade. This is not to discourage you as a trader but rather to lift you. Having such reminders will help you foresee the recurrence of past errors. It helps you amend those errors.

Regularly check on price volatility, the direction the trade is currently on, and market trends. You should also check the momentum of the trade and divergence. You also need to focus on your schedule of trade. The first three hours can significantly be utilized to build momentum.

You need to have it in mind that the market will always positively reinforce you for your disciple. This will be done by counting profits and continuous money flow. Trade discipline provides you with a larger and greater chance for profit. Often you should strive to become a winner in this corporate world. Ensure you work for your trade to be highest in the ladder. You need to secure and protect your profits.

You also need to follow trade methods that have been proven. These methods are not to be changed. If you try a methodology that is not proven and doesn't seem to work in some session of trade, don't just wake up in the morning and come up with another one. Find a proven method of trade that productively works for you and strictly go by it.

Besides, you are not required to chase markets. Patiently wait as it sets up. The market is equivalent to a shadow as following it will lead you nowhere as you can never reach for it. But if you are still, it will settle on you. Understand that this is a process; each step pushes you closer to achieving your goals and objectives. Do not make any haste. Decisions Research on ways you can increase your profits and reduce your losses.

Mastery of these guidelines will see you through in becoming a disciplined trader and working on your emotions. These emotions are not all bad can be used to give out positive results.

How can we manage our emotions to good suite us and our trade? This is known as Emotional Intelligence (EI). How do we improve our emotional quotient to work for us in this trade? You first need to be aware of your qualities; your strengths and your weaknesses have them in control. First, we need to be aware of the components of emotional intelligence, which are distinct, namely, social skills, self-awareness, self-regulation, empathy, and intrinsic motivation.

Having control of EI will improve your trade satisfaction and improved performances those under you will benefit from your knowledge. It is also good when encountering failures. Having on self-awareness of how your emotions work will help you control them and think of how you can possibly restructure your behavior. This would be difficult for traders who constantly have control of these situations. The most often have high self-esteem, and it will take them a long time to accept that this time around, they have lost control. They will end up giving negative feedback in their response.

You should not wait for an emotional crisis to emerge for you to alienate your feelings. You should not even eliminate them; doing so will make you emotionally unintelligent, and you just need to be ready for the game changers and how to react on them, possibly. Traders experience emotion, and a lack of emotion can prove to be fatal as it can kill the desire to act. While if you are unable to control your emotional reaction on excessive pain, you can easily blind how you think rationally and easily crowd your judgment.

Chapter 19. What Kind of Trader Are You?

There are all kinds of people who trade on the foreign exchange; from business executives to housewives, from government officials to students. Anyone who has the wherewithal to take on the fast-paced movement of an activity, the risks and the unpredictability can do it. It is the market of all markets.

Each class of trader has their own goals and expectations from the market, and while there is no clear-cut list of requirements, where you fall on this list will depend mainly on your risk assessment, the amount of time you want to prepare, and a long list of other factors.

The Scalper

Scalpers are fast movers. They enter the market quickly and just as quickly move out. They tend to hold their trades for concise periods, sometimes only for a few seconds before they try to sell again. The scalper uses the market's volatility to their advantage. Get in, get out, and repeat. This pattern is likely to be repeated many times throughout a single day.

Interestingly enough, they make considerably smaller trades in comparison to other traders. Their means of profits, however, are primarily due to their frequency of trading rather than from holding investments for a more extended period. To be an active scalper, there are specific characteristics that you must embrace.

- You must be able to make decisions at a moment's notice.

- You must have a strong emotional constitution to keep you from getting attached to the trade.

- You must function more like a machine when you're in trading mode.

- You must be able to accept losses quickly and move on to the next trade and not dwell on the negative.

Strategies that Scalpers Use when Trading

Scalpers know how to make quick profits and move on. To do this, they may mix and match several systems to get the job done. It is not unusual to see them scoping out 1-5-minute time frames on a chart in search of that quick buck. The term 'scalping' is often used to refer to the regularly 'skimming' of small profits.

Their approach to trade seems very chaotic as they are in a constant search for the next quick profit turnover. They often refer to tick charts, 5-minute, or 1-minute charts to get the indicators they need. Some seek out high-velocity moves in the socio-economic arenas that can have an impact on the movement of prices. For example, releases of the nation's employment statistics or GDP numbers trigger a huge reaction on the market, and the scalper is usually poised to take advantage of such announcements.

Why Scalp?

The scalper's strategy is to glean 5 to 10 PIPs from every trade. By repeating this process throughout the day, using high leverages, the profits can really mount up. Think about it, with a standard lot, and the average PIP is valued at around $10. That means that if they are successful in the skimming of 5 PIPs per trade and they do this ten times a day, they are earning at least $500/day, a very profitable return for a part-time trader.

Who Scalps?

Scalping is not a skill that anyone can develop. You need to have very distinct characteristics to be a good scalper.

- You must love sitting in front of the computer. You will have to sit there for hours on end.

- You must be able to hold your concentration for long periods, so you don't miss even the slightest opportunity. The opening may only be available for a few seconds before it disappears.

- You must be able to react quickly and not overthink every move. Scalpers do everything fast; analyzing every move could slow you down, and you'd lose many opportunities to trade and turn a profit.

Scalping Strategy

Like all Forex trades, research is at the very core of your career. While Forex is an international market, it is still unregulated, so it is up to you to know how much margin is required and what your options are in case of a loss.

While you can trade on your own through a trading platform, it is highly recommended that you use a broker to facilitate the trades for you. Many offer exclusive extras that can assure you get on the right path to success. Still, the platforms that one broker uses can be very different from other platforms, so learn all you can about them, even missing one detail could turn out to be very costly.

Liquidity

Scalpers look for the most liquid markets, which are usually found in the major currency pairs. Even among the primary currency pairs, some currencies tend to be more liquid than others. The best time to trade these markets is when they overlap. It is the time when you find the potential for higher profits.

Insurance

Scalpers always make sure they have more than one escape route. Most work online, and they need to react fast. What is your alternate plan for exiting a trade if you lose Internet connectivity? This is why working with a broker is beneficial. If something goes wrong, your broker can step in and close the transaction. They also have on hand other plans that can get them out of a trade quickly.

One of the main rules for scalpers is to look for trends in the charts. They usually use 5-minute and 1-minute charts to find the best times to enter and exit a trade. They are always looking for trends. They first study the 5-minute chart to find the current trend. There is a saying among traders on the Forex Market. A Trend is Your Friend, and there is no place where this truth exists than on the Forex Market. Keep in mind that there is psychology involved in market movement, and it is the psychology that determines much of the activity that leads to these trends.

It is essential to know how to identify these trends if you want to be effective at technical analysis. As a general rule, if an investor has found an uptrend, they will stick it out while they look for any sign that it's going to reverse. When that sign appears, they quickly exit the trade and walk away with their profit. The primary trends they are looking for are bullish and bearish, but there are at least three possible trends that they need to know about.

The Bullish Trend

To find the bullish trend using the 5-minute charts, look for candles that are making higher highs and higher lows. Check the price – If it is more than 5-EMA (Exponential Moving Average), then it is a bullish trend. Once you've found the bullish trend look for the same trend on the 1-minute chart. Search for a reversal candle (this may be formed after a correction in price.

If you find the reversal candle (it could also be called a hammer, doji, morning star) on the 1-minute chart, they enter the trade above the closing price for that candle. Make sure the stop-loss is only a few PIPs down from the reversal candle. Finally, exit the trade after the 1-minute candle closes below the 15-EMA.

The Bearish Trend

To find the bearish trend, follow the same steps as listed above but instead check for the lower lows first on the 5-minute chart and then again on the 1-minute chart. If the lower highs are below the 5-EMA mark, then it is bearish. Another option is to look at the current price. If it is below the 5-EMA on the 5-minute chart, then you can conclude it is bearish.

Once you've determined that the short-term trends are bearish, do a search for similar entries based on the 1-minute chart. Find the bearish reversal candle on the 1-minute chart. It should be located after a pullback or a price reversal. Enter the trade just underneath the closing price of the reversal candle. Place the stop-loss only a few PIPs above the high of the reversal candle. Exit the trade when the 1-minute candle closes above the 15-EMA.

The Neutral Trend

The only trend a scalper wants to avoid is the neutral trend. These trends are neither bullish nor bearish.

The Intraday Traders

The Intraday Trader doesn't work as fast as the Scalper. They usually hold their trades for a little longer.

While they may make some trades that last only a few minutes, it is not uncommon for them to hold onto them for a few hours. Because of this, they make fewer trades per day, but the flip side is that they can turn higher profits or losses with every trade.

Intraday trading happens when there is a position that can be opened and liquidated within a typical trading day. It is considered to be one of the most difficult kinds of trade you can do yet it is very popular for several reasons.

- The small size of the investment

- The ability to gain huge advantages from margin trading and leverage

- The ability to take on several positions throughout the day

- It has the potential to be more profitable than long-term trading

The Intraday Trader has a tough challenge in that numerous market noises, and daily fluctuations often influence the results of his market.

Therefore, all traders need to be sharp enough to catch the small fluctuations that can range from as little as a few PIPs to as many as a few hundred. Just like other traders in the market, the sole purpose of the Intraday Trader is to earn profits. Their ultimate goal is to take advantage of the fluctuations in the prices to make more money.

The Intraday Personality

Independent: Most traders work from home without someone telling them what to do or when to do it. To be successful, you have to be self-motivated and thrive in a controlled setting.

Decisive: This type of trader needs to make decisions fast. Since the market can change quickly, a good trader must be able to process information quickly and come to a decision. They rely a lot on their own experience but also from having a good understanding of research and preparation before coming up with a strategy.

Disciplined: They need to stay on task even when there are distractions around them. They are determined enough to come up with a plan and stick with it until it no longer works to their benefit.

Open-Minded: Traders need to follow profitable strategies to their conclusion, even if they don't see immediate results. They are willing to try several strategies one right after another, continually improving their technique until they find what works best for their situation.

Technically Savvy: This does not mean you have to be an expert at computer programming, but you should be able to know how to navigate a trading software program effectively and be willing to try new programs as they become available. Bottom line, you need to stay well ahead of the curve.

Financially Secure: While they don't have to be independently wealthy, they do have to have enough liquidity to be able to trade and cover their losses. They should always keep some reserve cash on hand just in case.

Chapter 20. Why You Should Practice Day Trading

You couldn't wait to go home so you could open the package and start playing. The instruction manual may also have been part of the plastic wrap that was discarded seconds after opening. Well, take those memories and keep them good, because you cannot take the same approach with day trading. Day trading is one of, if not the most difficult things you will undertake in your life. So, having to practice shouldn't come as a surprise. Below, I will cover the ten reasons why you should practice day trading.

Day Trading is Super-Fast

Talk about knocking it down first in the post, but the daily trade is very fast. If you think about chess, what is one way you can increase the chess difficulty level? Put a stopwatch on how long you need to make a move. This is where true skill emerges because intuition, experience, and repetition come into play. Well, the market is no different. If I have a few days to analyze a position, I can work out a good trading plan with notes for myself. When operating during the day, it can only take a few minutes to a few seconds to make a decision. So you think chess players start playing with a 1-minute timer, obviously not. Therefore, you shouldn't even end up on the market with your hard-earned money, trying to make some harmless transactions. Take time to practice day trading to develop the skills necessary to enter the field.

Practice Day Trading in Response to the Market

The market is a true living being. While you have a history of some price movements, each day is unique. You'll have to see how you react to it when the tape airs and the actions move. It's one thing to just look at the old charts, but you have to get used to listening to the market. Much of day trade is intuition. This is the part of your trading toolbox that you cannot quantify, and it is unique to you and your trading style.

Learn to Manage Your Money

One thing I say is that I cannot practice day trading on a simulator because it is not real money. To some extent, this is true. But let me ask you, did you have fire drills at your school when you were a child, even if there was no real fire? But if there was a fire, did you know where to go? Did you know what path you should follow to get out of the building? Did your teachers know how long it would take to get all the children out? Did the firefighter expect where to be within a certain period?

You have to get used to calculate the gains and losses in your head. You must learn to trade effectively on margin. Risk compensation ratios must be evaluated quickly, and only the best opportunities should be run, as there are five to choose from at the same time. Now, you can read this and say, well, it's not real money yet, so I'm not going to take it seriously, and you know what, you reserve the right to make that adult decision. But I always want to know what to do in case of fire.

Find Out How to Manage Winning and Losing Trades

Trading is great when you are making money. The beauty of being in this losing position is that it quickly humiliated me in a matter of days. The key thing I know and will learn to develop over time is that you must forget the losers and winners the moment you close your position. Bringing your grudges to the next operation will only harm you because there are new market participants in every action. Therefore, practicing trade allows you to speed up the pace. When I say rhythm, I mean the negotiation cycle. Some win, others lose, but you must learn to deal with every trade with a positive mindset and sound trading principles. This is another one of those skill sets that come from pure repetition. You just have to make a horrible trade just to follow 15 direct winners to realize that the bad trade doesn't require you to start psychoanalyzing your infancy.

You Need Your 10,000 Hours of Practice

I know, I know, so, I'll keep it short. Studies have shown that you need to practice something for 10,000 hours before you become an expert. Think about your jobs or careers. If you are an executive, employers require 10 to 15 years of job search experience. If you do simple math, a full-time equivalent per year is 2.00 hours. So, if you think about it, employers are saying you should have 20,000 to 30,000 hours of experience before allowing you to run a department. Well, guess what; the same is true for the trading day. Overtime training will allow you to exponentially increase the time required to reach that 10,000 hours expert level.

Know that All Charts Don't Go to the Moon

Earlier in my career, I would have scoured the market for specific configurations that would have made big profits. I would identify a particular model with the same indicators to find that weak point. After configuring my settings, historically, these winning rankings seemed to be everywhere. Day trading today is done with computers, and the level of ongoing games in terms of fake breakouts is insane. What taught me to practice day trading is that it is more important to reserve the earnings of singles than to always swing by the fences. These take me to the moon setting; they will only pay 10% to 20% of the time, so stop waiting for it to happen every time you trade. Focus on the rhythm of just winning, and when the big trade comes, you'll know it.

Discover Your Day Trading Style

I believe that as adults, we are responsible for our decisions in life. Don't blame your parents or some events that happened to you in third grade for why you do certain things in your life. I'm not trying to rule out the impact of life experiences, but what I'm saying is that we can choose how long we let them influence how we live our lives. Well, for day trading, I think, for the most part, it's easier not to "take over" your trading strategy and leave it to the expert. Most people will go in and fight to put together a system: paralysis analysis at its best. So go to Google, do some searching and voila, there is your friendly "day trade expert" ready to sell you the magic keys to your promise land. I am not judging you; I have spent thousands on other people's courses, hoping to find myself. What I realized is that these courses are other people's rules. Trading requires that you understand what works for you.

Guess what, people, it's work. It will take thousands of hours to modify and re-optimize to understand what corresponds to your business DNA. The reason I chose to go my way was when these systems started to fail, who did I start blaming? You guessed it right, the man behind the curtain who sold me this wonderful course. Stop this vicious circle today.

When these courses make you win, everything is fantastic, but since you don't really understand all the rules, when things go wrong, you lose your confidence. Please do me a favor and skip all this pain. I'm not saying that you can't collect key principles from other day traders, but you have to define your methodology yourself. Only you can do it, so when things go wrong, you don't blame mom or dad, you look in the mirror.

You Need More Reps

If you've ever tried for a sports team, practices are only for a certain period each day. Therefore, you only have a limited window to show your coach that you have what it takes to be a team member. Since we only exchange buds in the morning, I have a maximum of 2-4 exchanges that I can do on any given day. It would take me a little over two months to have 100 trades to analyze.

At first, one of my challenges was trying to figure out how well I was doing compared to myself daily. This allowed you to quickly create a trading plan that would have taken too long if you had tried to do it only during market hours. It has a significant impact on your ability to quickly change your performance-based trading strategy and ultimately leads to making more money.

Show Yourself You Can Be a Day Trader

Market research is none other than Monday's quarterback. You start to tell yourself, I would have been in that trade and would have made this sum of money. But you are looking back on the old lists of things that have already been played; however, in a market simulation environment, there is tremendous value to you, with real data that you have everything you need to make money. You must believe that regardless of your background, education or age, you can do it. If you practice day trading long enough, you will get to that point where you can tell yourself that I am a professional day trader. Work only by showing yourself that you can trade, and then watch how this will boost your confidence when the time comes to fight the big boys.

See How Long You Can Expect to Do Daily Operations

The better way is to see yourself than to go to a simulator and start the account balance with the money at hand, depending on your system and how long you have it, it can take a few weeks or months to swap a full calendar year. At the end of the year, after considering fees and living expenses, how much money do you have left? Practicing day trading can begin to answer some of these confusing aspects of day trading.

Chapter 21. Working Mechanisms of Inter Bank Currency Markets

Like other goods, the currency is also bought and sold in markets, which is known as the foreign exchange market. The top three most communal transactions in the world are exchanges between the dollar and the euro 30 percent, the dollar and the yen 20 percent, and the dollar and pound 12 percent.

Factors Including Inter Bank Currency Markets

The Demand for Currency

The market for currencies is consequent from a country's Demand for exports, and from investors trying to benefit from currency value changes.

The Supply of Currency

The domestic demand for foreign imports determines the availability of currency. For instance, when the U.K. imports cars from Japan, they have to pay in yen and sell pounds to buy yen. The more it imports into the foreign exchange market, the larger the supply of pounds. A substantial proportion of short-term currency trading is by traders who work for financial institutes. The foreign exchange market of London is the single biggest currency exchange market in the whole world.

Exchange Rates and Interest Rates

Fluctuations in the interest rates of a nation also disturb its currency because of its effect on the Demand and supply of financial resources in the U.K. and abroad. For instance, high-interest rates compared to other countries make U.K. business-friendly to stakeholders, leading to higher Demand for U.K.'s financial resources and higher Demand for Pound Sterling.

On the other hand, lower interest duties in one country compared to other countries contribute to higher supply, as speculators sell currency to buy currencies connected with higher interest rates. Such hypothetical flows are called hot money and have an essential influence on exchange rates in the short run.

Supply and Demand in Currency Markets

Supply and Demand run the foreign exchange or Forex market, much like every other market in the world. Indeed, knowing the idea of supply and Demand in the Forex market is so critical that we can take a step back into Economics 101 for a minute to make sure we are all on the same page. Having a firm knowledge of supply and Demand would make all the difference in your Forex investment career because it will give you the prospect to search through the daily news mountain and find the most exciting messages. And how does the Forex market is affected by both supply and Demand?

Supply is the indicator of how much of a given product at any particular time is accessible. The value of a product, in this case, a currency, is directly connected to its production. The currency would get less cost, with the currency supply rising. On the other hand, money becomes more valuable as the currency supply drops.

Think of diamonds and rocks. Since rocks are everywhere, they are not useful. You can walk along a country path and pick from hundreds or even thousands of rocks. On the other side, diamonds are costly because many of them are not on track. A limited volume of diamonds is available internationally, so if you like it, you have to offer a fee.

We find Demand, on the other hand, of the economic calculation. Demand is the indicator of how much customers desire to buy one particular product at any particular moment. Currency demand has the reverse impact on currency value than availability. The currency gets more expensive as the market for a currency rises. Alternatively, the currency is less competitive as Demand for a currency decline.

You just have to look at Tickle Me Elmo to get a clear sense of the impact demand may have on anything's price. Upon the first appearance of Tickle Me Elmo, the market for the product was insane. Parents trampled on each other so anyone else could wipe Elmo off their arms and make sure that they both got on their kid's list. To those not fast or competitive enough to bring Tickle Me, Elmo, from the market, it was their last resort to pay outrageously high rates on eBay. This giant red giggling doll had become a tremendous demand far more desirable than it would have been if no one's girl had desired it.

So, the trick to be effective in the currency market is to know about where the supply on the market is increasing and where Demand is rising. In this competitive industry, if you can choose that, you are well on your way to making a huge profit. We consider utilizing the "seesaw of supply and demand" to show yourself a very good view of what is happening in the money market environment. And it is with one currency that influences each currency pair you are willing to exchange that is the best way to start this: U.S. dollar.

The Seesaw of Supply and Demand

Supply and Demand have two sides to them. The left side reflects rising Demand and declining supply. When evaluating the dollar to see how strong or how vulnerable it is in the future, you have to remember all the essential factors of the seesaw. If Demand rises or rising stocks, a basic element is put on the left side of the seesaw. You must stack it on the right side of the panel if a critical element improves output or reduces Demand. You may notice it starts to tip up or down as you put more and more essential factors on the seesaw based on how many essential factors there are on each side.

If the left side of the seesaw has more influence, the left side will fall while the right-side increases. When this occurs, you know this, practically speaking; the value of the U.S. dollar will rise. One speedy way to note this is to look at the seesaw's slope. You can see it ascends from left to right.

The supply and demand seesaw will enable you to synthesize the more understandable type of complicated economic knowledge. For instance, evaluating the overall relative strength of the U.S. dollar makes it simple to sidetrack and lose as you seek to follow different variables, such as unemployment, trade balance, levels of interest, and so forth, which impact the value of the U.S. dollar. But, when looking at each of these variables independently, it is far simpler to determine if each element has a favorable or detrimental effect on the valuation of the U.S. dollar in a vacuum.

When a factor has been assessed, put it on the accurate side of the seesaw, and move on to the next element. When you go through the various factors impacting the value of the U.S. currency, you may begin to see which side of the seesaw is overwhelmed, and you can develop either a bias of the strong-dollar or bias of the weak-dollar. That is a great way to get your essential research going.

What Is Inflation-Interest-Relationship?

Inflation and interest rates are frequently correlated in macroeconomics and often cited. Inflation refers to the extent to which the products and services prices upsurge. In the USA, the interest rate, or the amount paid to a borrower by a lender, is based on the rate of federal funds set by the Federal Reserve, sometimes called "the Fed".

Through setting the target for the federal funds rate, the Fed has at its fingertips a powerful tool that it utilizes to control the rate of inflation. This instrument allows the Fed to extend or contract the money supply if required to achieve target employment rates, stability in prices, and stable economic development.

The Correlation Between Interest Rates and Inflation

The interest rates and inflation continue to be inversely correlated in a regime of fractional reserve banking. This association forms one of the contemporary monetary policy's core tenets: Central banks control short-term interest rates to impact the economy's inflation rate.

The chart below displays the inverse relation of interest rates to inflation. CPI refers, in the table, to the Consumer Price Index, a metric that calculates market changes. Changes in the CPI help to measure periods of inflation and deflation.

When interest rates are increasingly reduced, more people can borrow more money. The result is that clients have more money to spend, improving the economy and rising inflation. For increasing interest rates, the converse holds. When interest rates upsurge, customers continue to invest when savings levels grow. With the rise in the interest rate consuming less disposable income, the economy slows, and inflation falls.

It is necessary to understand the banking system, the monetary theory of money and the position of interest rates to understand better how the correlation between inflation and interest rates works.

The Importance of Inflation and GDP

Fractional Reserve Banking

A fractional reserve banking scheme is extensively used in the world. When anyone is putting $100 into the bank, they hold a claim on that $100. However, the bank will lend out those dollars based on the central bank's reserve ratio. If the reserve is 10%, the bank would be able to lend the other 90%, which in this case is $90. A percentage of the capital stays in the bank vaults at 10 percent.

As long as the subsequent $90 loan remains unpaid, the economy has two statements that equal $190. In other words, the money supply went up from $100 to $190. It is a clear example of how the money supply increases with banking.

Quality Theory of Money

In economics, the quality theory of money describes that the supply and Demand for money determine inflation. If the supply of money increases, prices continue to increase, as any single piece of paper is less valuable.

Hyperinflation is an economic concept used to characterize severe inflation in situations of quick and unchecked rises in costs. While central banks typically look for a decent annual inflation rate of around 2% to 3%, hyperinflation goes even further than that. Hyperinflation nations had an inflation rate of 50% or higher every month.

Interest Rates, Savings, Loans, and Inflation

The interest rate serves as a price to keep or lend money. To attract investors, banks pay an interest rate on deposits. Banks often earn the interest rate on their deposits for income.

If interest rates are low, individuals and businesses continue to make more loans. Within a fractional reserve banking structure, any banking loan would raise monetary supply. The quantity theory of money indicates how a growing availability of currency raises inflation. High-interest rates also continue to contribute to further inflation. Inflation is weaker despite elevated interest levels. This is a simplistic view of the relationship, but it underlines why interest rates and inflation continue to converge inversely.

The Role of the Committee of Federal Open Market

FOMC Federal Open Market Committee meets eight times a year to study and vote on monetary policy and economic and financial conditions. The monetary policy applies to acts that influence the money and credit supply and costs. Short-term interest rate thresholds are set at those meetings.

Chapter 22. About Options Markets

In your trading, some of the concepts involved are background material that won't impact your actual day-to-day trading. We will also talk about brokers and commissions as well, which is going to be more impactful.

Options are Derivatives Contracts

Options are a type of derivative contract. You may have first heard about "derivatives" during the 2008 housing market crash. But don't let the term scare you. Derivative simply means that the value of financial security is derived from an underlying asset.

Options Exchanges

Just like stocks, options are traded on exchanges. There are many options exchanges. The largest options market is owned by NASDAQ, which, as you probably know, is a stock market that is mainly made up of technology stocks. NASDAQ owns six different options exchanges. These include the Nasdaq Options Market, PHLX, BZX, Gemini, Mercury, and ISE. Together, the six options exchanges owned by NASDAQ make up about a third of total options trading. Another major options exchange is CBOE/BATS.

As a trader, the options exchanges are hidden from you. Trading options, like trading stocks, will be presented to you in an electronic format that is completely unified, and the actual exchange where the option is bought or sold is invisible. Your broker creates the interface between you and the options exchanges. So while it may be good to at least know about the options exchanges, this is not something you have to become an expert on to trade options or to make a profit trading option. You won't even be aware of the exchanges themselves as you go about your business.

Options Clearing Corporation

The options clearing corporation or OCC is an organization that issues and guarantees options contracts. The OCC is regulated by the U.S. Securities and Exchange Commission or SEC. The OCC manages transactions involving call and put options. They are also involved with futures contracts. The main function of the options clearing corporation is to ensure that the obligations outlined in options contracts are fulfilled by working with brokers. The organization also helps provide regulatory oversight of the options markets to help manage risk.

Market Maker

Options market makers are under contract with options exchanges to help provide liquidity in the options markets. These are professional traders that are paid by the exchanges to fulfill this role. They can be large institutional traders or even individuals. The main purpose of market makers is to ensure that retail traders can trade options. Market makers will often take the other side of your trades. They maintain a large inventory of financial assets of their own and often use actual stock trades to hedge their risk in taking options trades that have a certain probability of being a losing trade. Market makers are viewing the markets in a completely different way than individual traders, such as you view the market.

This fact is because they are not focused on individual trades. They are focused on the aggregate of large numbers of trades and overall probabilities. When you are trading, you aren't going to know who takes the other side of the trade, and it's not relevant. It might be another retail trader, it could be an institution, or it might be the market maker. Your only focus when trading is on the performance of the stock, entering and exiting trades in a way that works for your situation. Market makers have huge portfolios of options contracts that are known as "inventory". If you are trading a low volume option, the market maker can help keep the market liquid by taking the other side of the trade.

The Options Industry Council

The Options Industry Council or OIC is an educational organization. It is sponsored by many options exchanges, and its main purpose is to educate the public about options trading. They also have an online store where you can buy videos, books, and software. This site is highly recommended for use to further your education in options trading. You should use these reliable and official course materials rather than relying on online gurus who have other, sometimes, ulterior motives.

Virtual Trading Platforms

It will allow you to engage in demo options trades so that you can gain experience without risking any money. The demo trades operate as real trades except for real money is on the line, so you can go through trades and learn how things work with no real risk. Since options trading can be quite tricky and different from stock trading, using this procedure is highly recommended, at least for a short period. Many people are impatient and want to dig into real trading right away, but if you prepare yourself by spending a few weeks or a month using a demo trading platform, you are going to be better off than someone who starts the gate risking their funds. Do some research online to find a broker that has a practice trading platform. Some examples include swim, which is operated by the famous stockbroker TD Ameritrade, and another one you can use is run by a company called Tasty Works.

The Broker

Just like you need a broker to trade stocks as an individual investor, you need a broker to trade options. Since options are closely associated with the stock market, the same brokers that are used for trading stocks are involved in options trading.

What is a broker? A broker is simply a middleman. As an individual trader, you are not going to go through the work of finding where a specific option is traded and then trade on the exchange. Instead, everything is hidden from you by the broker who does the actual legwork. Of course, these days, everything is managed electronically, and so the broker will present you with the options exchanges as if it were one single, unified market. They play the role of acting between you as the individual trader and the exchange and whoever takes the opposite side of the trade.

With today's computational power and fully electronic trading, everything runs seamlessly. Behind the scenes, you place an order with your broker, and the broker carries out the trade on your behalf. Since the broker is doing work for you, they will often charge a fee for placing each trade that is called a commission. Not all options brokers charge commissions, and they make money in other ways.

The broker will provide a software interface that you can use for options trading. Some brokers provide a basic interface that will allow you to look up options and place your trades, while others will also include the ability to do in-depth analysis. These days most brokers make their interface available through the internet on desktop computers or as mobile applications for tablets and mobile phones. Finding a good balance between features offered by the broker and fees like commissions is important. If you are using a broker that does charge commissions, this is going to be something that you have to figure into all of your trades when calculating profits and losses.

Tasty Works is one of the most popular options trading platforms. Pit traders started it from the Chicago exchanges, and so it's run by people that know the business. They also have an associated educational network called tasty trades that helps educate people and keep them informed, often including interviews with successful options traders. Tasty works charge small commissions, on the order of $1 per option contract. We will learn about more complicated options strategies that involve multiple options in a single trade. Each option is known as a "leg," so if you have two options in a single trade, that is a 2-leg trade, while a trade involving four options has four legs.

When selecting a broker, you are also going to want to know about any charges associated with the legs. Tasty works will charge a maximum of $10 per leg. Single leg trades are $1 each, but as of 2018, the company allows you to open 100 calls or puts for just $10. As of 2018, they also lowered their prices for 100 vertical two leg options to $20, and 100 4 leg trades were capped at $40. So the price of $10 per leg is for 100 options contracts. They also only charge commissions on opening an options trade, and there is zero commission charged on closing options trades.

Robinhood has become a very popular trading platform. While you can access it through a desktop computer, it's mainly designed to run as a mobile app. Robinhood is very popular because it has a clean, simple trading interface, and it also charges zero commissions. Many experienced traders don't like Robinhood because it has some downsides. The most important downside for most traders is that it has limited information available as far as tools used for analysis. However, you can get that type of information elsewhere, so you might look at it as a tradeoff that you are willing to accept to get commission-free trades.

Traditional stockbrokers offer options trading as well. These include Charles Schwab, E*Trade, and TD Ameritrade. Ultimately the broker you choose is a personal decision, so you should evaluate each broker you may be interested in and find the one you prefer, rather than doing what others tell you to do.

Once you find your broker, you can fund your account. This is done by linking a bank account to the account maintained by your broker and depositing some funds into the account. You can trade options contracts one at a time, so you only need to fund an account with a couple of hundred dollars to get started. I advise that beginners start slowly and small, don't jump in and buy 20 call options right away. Do one contract at a time so that you can learn how to trade options before putting significant money at risk.

Options vs. Stocks

The main advantage of options over stocks is that options provide leverage and a massively higher return on investment. We touched on this earlier. You can invest a much smaller amount of money and earn profits that are similar in magnitude to what you would earn trading 100 shares of stock, but without having to put thousands of dollars at risk. For those who don't have thousands of dollars to put at risk trading, options offer a way for them to take advantage of price swings in the market.

Consider a stock trading at $200 a share. If you were to buy 100 shares of stock, that would require an investment of $20,000. Now suppose that the stock rises by $2 a share. That would give you a total of $200 in profit, not accounting for commissions. So you could sell the 100 shares and take your profits. Of course, $200 profit from one trade is a good take.

Chapter 23. Fundamental Analysis

This is where proper analysis comes into play either through technical analysis (outlined below) or via fundamental analysis. Fundamental analysis is used more frequently by new traders, while technical analysis has experienced something of a renaissance in popularity over the past decade or so. While both are useful when it comes to finding the information you are looking for, they go about determining just what that information is in different ways. Fundamental analysis is primarily concerned with looking at the big picture, which often means that it will take longer to perform than its counterpart.

Additionally, its information comes from external sources, which means you may need to wait for additional information to become available through it will typically end up being easier to digest than the information required utilizing technical analysis effectively. Broadly, the fundamental analysis makes it easier for you to glimpse the likely future of the forex market based on a wide variety of different variables, including publicized changes to the monetary policy of the countries you are interested in. The end goal is to track down enough information to allow you to find an undervalued currency pair that the market has not adjusted to.

Determine the Baseline

When it comes to considering the fundamental aspects of a currency pair, you will first want to consider the baseline that these currencies typically return to time after time when compared to the other currency pairs that are commonly traded. It will make it easier to determine when the right time to make a move is likely to be as you will then be more easily able to pinpoint changes that occur to the pair that make them warrant additional consideration.

To determine this baseline, the first thing you will need to consider is any changes to the related macroeconomic policy that affects each based on historical data. In these instances, past behavior is one of the most reliable indicators when it comes to determining likely future events. Once you are aware of the relevant historical context, you will then need to consider the current phase that the currency is in and how likely it is to remain in the phase-in question as opposed to moving on to the next.

Each currency regularly goes through 6 distinct phases, the first of which is the boom phase, which can be identified via low volatility and large amounts of liquidity. At the opposite end of the spectrum is the bust phase, which can be identified by the opposite, mainly low amounts of liquidity and high amounts of volatility. The other phases are post-bust and pre-bust and post-boom and pre-boom, which means that one of the major phases is either on its way in or on its way out. Determining the proper phase is crucial when it comes to ensuring that you are on the right track when it comes to finding a trading pair that is likely to be profitable in the long-term.

To determine the current phase, the easiest way to go about doing so is by looking at the current number of defaults along with bank loans as well as the accumulated reserve levels of the related currencies. If the numbers are low, then a boom phase is likely on its way or possibly in full swing already. If the current numbers have already overstayed their welcome, then you can be confident that a post-boom phase is likely to start at any time. Alternatively, if the numbers in question are higher than the baseline you have already established, then you know that the currency is likely either due for a bust phase or is already underway.

Money can be made regardless of the current phase as long as you can capitalize on it before the market catches up as it is typically fairly slow-moving.

Worldwide Considerations

After you have an understanding of the baseline, the currency pairs you are working with tend to remain at. The next thing you will want to do is to determine is what the related global economic conditions are likely to be and how they are going to affect your trading pair. One of the best ways to go about doing so is to looking into emerging technologies in the related countries as they can easily turn entire economies on their heads in a relatively short time.

After it reaches the saturation point, then you are going to want to be on the lookout for the bust phase as it will likely be right around the corner. If you feel as though the countries related to the currencies in question will soon be in a post-bust or post-boom phase, then you will want to think twice about moving into speculative markets as the drop off is sure to become, and it can be difficult to determine exactly when it will rear its ugly head.

If you feel confident that a phase shift is on the horizon, but you don't know when it will be exactly, then you are going to want to stick with smaller leverage points than you would during the other phases to ensure that they will pay out before the change occurs. On the other hand, if a phase is just starting, then you will want to go ahead and make riskier trades as the time concerns aren't going to come into play, which means extra caution is less warranted.

Global Implications

While it might be difficult to determine where you should start, at first, all you need to do is to apply the same level of analysis that you have performed on the micro-level, just on a larger scale. The best place to start is generally going to be with the interest rates of the major players on the world stage include the Federal Reserve, the European Central Bank, the Bank of England and the Bank of Japan.

You will also need to be aware of any policy biases of legal mandates that are currently making the rounds to ensure that you don't end up getting blindsided from these sources when it comes time for you to make your move. While this will certainly be time-consuming work, understanding the market from all sides will make it easier to determine new emerging markets when specific areas are fat with supply growth and what the expectations regarding interest rate changes or market volatility are soon going to be.

Understand the Past

After you have a clear idea of what the current state of the worldwide economy is looking like, along with the specifics regarding the currency pairs you are interested in trading, then the next thing you will need to do is look to the past so that you can be prepared for history to repeat itself. This level of understanding will make it easier for you to understand the current strength of your respective currencies while also allowing you to more accurately determine the length of time you can expect the current phase to continue.

To capitalize on this knowledge in the most effective way possible, you are going to want to attempt to jump onto trades when one of the currencies is entering a post-bust phase while the other is in the midst of a post-boom phase. When this occurs, credit channels will not yet be exhausted, and you will be able to take advantage of the greatest amount of risk possible when compared to any other market state.

Be Aware of Volatility

Being aware of the current level of volatility is crucial when it comes to ensuring that the investments you are making are likely to payout in your favor.

This is relatively easy to do; all you need to do is to pay attention to the stock markets most closely related to the currencies your favor. It is because the forex market tends to be more stable, the more stable the stock market is because the lower the perceived overall risk is, the lower the amount of perceived risk that can make its way to the forex market.

Remember, the closer to the peak of the boom phase you currently find yourself, the lower interest rates, default rates, and volatility will be, which means it is the best time to increase your level of risk.

Alternately, the closer you find yourself to the bust phase, the higher the overall level of volatility, default and interest rates are going to be.

Decide on the Best Currency Pairs

With a good idea of where the market currently is and how long it is likely to stay there, all that you have left to do is determine the most effective currency pairs actually to sell. To do this, you must first consider any gap between the two currencies when it comes to interest rates.

To find this information, you are going to want to start by looking at the difference in the output gap as well as related unemployment statistics. When capacity constraints increase, while at the same time, unemployment decreases, this shortage will lead to an inflated economy, which in turn, will cause interest rates will rise until the economy begins to cool? Charting this information will allow you to accurately determine the likely interest rate movement from the pair in question.

Additionally, you will want to consider the payment balance of the nations related to the currencies in question.

The healthier the debt to capital ratio, the stronger the related currency is likely to remain in times of crisis. To determine this amount, you are going to want to consider the capital as well as the current account and the general situation of each. This will help you to determine if the position the nation in question is holding is due to asset sales or bank deposits or other, long term potential developments, including things like an accumulation of reserves or foreign investment.

Economic Indicators to Watch

When it comes to major economic indicators, the list is a fairly short one. Unfortunately, if you hope to stay competitive in the forex market, then you are going to need to keep up with far more than just the basics.

This is easier said than done, however, as there are a huge variety of economic surveys and other relevant indicators that can be used to predict numerous types of trends before they happen.

It is because rather than simply present the reader with raw data, it instead uses a tone that is much more conversational as it describes the various regional goings-on of the various members of the United States Federal banking districts.

This allows traders to determine how the Fed comes to various conclusions in various circumstances, which, in turn, can be useful later on when it comes to making bets on how the currency will move in the future.

This economic indicator is published before each Federal Open Market Committee Meeting, which works out to be eight times per year.

Chapter 24. Power Principles to Ensure a Strong Entry into Day Trading Options

I cannot stress this enough - you need to have a plan if you want to be successful at day trading options. You are putting your money on the line every day. I am sure squandering those hard-earned funds is not the plan, but that is what will exactly happen without a proper plan in place. Think of that trading plan as the foundation of your house of success. The principles that we will discuss below are the bricks to develop your house into what you want it to be.

Power Principle #1 – Ensure Good Money Management

Money is the tool that keeps the engine of the financial industry performing in good working order. You must learn to manage your money in a way that works for you instead of against you as an options day trader. It is an intricate part of managing your risk and increasing your profit.

Money management is the process whereby monies are allocated for spending, budgeting, saving, investing and other processes. Money management is a term that any person with a career in the financial industry, and particularly in the options trading industry, is intimately familiar with because this allocation of funds is the difference between a winning options trader and a struggling options trader. Below you will find tips for managing your money so that you have maximum control of your options day trading career.

Money Management Tips for Options Traders

Define money goals for the short term and the long term so that you can envision what you would like to save, invest, etc. Ensure that these are recorded and easily accessed. Your trading plan will help you define your money goals.

Use the position sizing to manage your money. To do this effectively, allocated a smart percentage of your investment fund toward individual options. For example, it would be unwise to use 50% of your investment fund on one option.

That is 50% of your capital that can potentially go down the drain if you make a loss in that position.

A good percentage is using no more than 10% of your investment fund toward individual option positions. This percentage allocation will help you get through tough periods, which eventually happen without having all your funds being lost.

Never, ever invest money that you cannot afford to lose. Do not let emotion override this principle and cloud your judgment.

Spread your risks by diversifying your portfolio. You diversify your portfolio by spreading your wealth by investing in different areas, add to your investments regularly, being aware of commissions at all times and knowing when to close a position.

Develop the day trading styles and strategies that earn you a steady rate of return. Even if you use scalping where the returns are comparatively small, that steady flow of profit can add up big over time.

Power Principle #2 – Ensure that Risks and Rewards Are Balanced

The risk/reward ratio is an assessment used to show profit potential about potential losses. This requires knowing the potential risks and profits associated with an options trade. Potential risks are managed by using a stop-loss order. A stop-loss order is a command that allows you to exit a position in an options trade once a certain price threshold has been reached.

Profit is targeted using an established plan. Potential profit is calculated by finding the difference between the entry price and the target profit.

Another way to manage risks and rewards is by diversifying your portfolio. Always spread your money across different assets, financial sectors and geographies. Ensure that these different facets of your portfolio are not closely related to each other so that if one goes down, they do not fall. Be smart about protecting and building your wealth.

Power Principle #3 – Develop a Consistent Monthly Options Trading System

The aim of doing options trading is to have an overall winning options trading month daily. That will not happen if you trade options here and there. You cannot expect to see a huge profit at the end of the month if you only performed 2 or 3 transactions.

You need to have a high options trading frequency to up the chances of coming out winning every month. To have consistently good months, you need to develop strong daily systems that keep your overall monthly average high.

Therefore, creating a daily options trading schedule is key. Here is an example of an efficient options day trading schedule.

Perform Market Analysis

This needs to be done before the markets open in the morning. That means that the options day trader needs to get an early start on the day. This entails checking the news to scan for any major events that might affect the markets that day, checking the economic calendar and assessing the actions of other day traders to assess volume and competition.

Manage Your Portfolio

The way that an options day trader does this is dependent on the strategies that he or she implements. Still, overall, it is about assessing positions that you already have or are contemplating for efficient management of entry and exits that day. It also allows for good money management.

Enter New Positions

After assessing the market and fine-tuning your portfolio, the next step is to enter new trades that day. Research and efficient decision-making go into this step. The options trader who has already determined how the market was doing and forecasted for performance that day would have noticed relevant patterns. The key here is to enter trades frequently via a sound strategy. To narrow done which positions you would like to pursue, keep an eye on the bullish, bearish, neutral and volatile watch lists and run technical scans.

Incorporate Learning During the Day

Continual learning is something that an option trader needs to pursue, but this does not always have to be in the way of formal classes or courses. You can up your knowledge of options and day trading by following mentors, reading books, listening to podcasts, reading blogs and watching videos online. Such activities are easy to incorporate into your daily routine. Even just a few minutes of study a day can go considerably up your options day trading game in addition to stimulating your mind. Being in regular contact with other options day traders is also a great way of increasing your information well.

Power Principle #4 – Consider a Brokerage Firm that Is Right for Your Level of Options Expertise

There are four important factors that you need to consider when choosing a broker, and they are:

- The requirements for opening a cash and margin account.

- The unique services and features that the broker offers.

- The commission fees and other fees charged by the broker.

- The reputation and level of options expertise of the broker.

Broker Cash and Margin Accounts

Every option trader needs to open a cash account and margin account to be able to perform transactions. They are simply tools of the trade. A cash account is one that allows an options day trader to perform transactions via being loaded with cash. Margin account facilitates transactions by allowing that to borrow money against the value of security in his or her account. Both of these types of accounts require that a minimum amount be deposited. This can be as few as a few thousand dollars to tens of thousands of dollars, depending on the broker of choice. You need to be aware of the requirements when deliberating, which brokerage firm is right for you.

Broker Services and Features

There are different types of services and features available from different brokerage firms. For example, if an options trader would like to have an individual broker assigned to him or her to handle his or her account personally, then he or she will have to look for a full-service broker. In this instance, there minimum account requirements that need to be met. Also, commission fees and other fees are generally higher with these types of brokerage firms. While the fees are higher, this might be better for a beginner trader to have that full service dedicated to their needs and the learning curve.

On the other hand, if an options trader does not have the capital needed to meet the minimum requirements of a full-service broker or would prefer to be more in charge of his or her option trades, then there is the choice of going with a discount brokerage firm. The advantage to discount brokerage firms is that they tend to have lower commissions and fees. Most internet brokerage firms are discount brokers.

Other features that you need to consider when choosing a brokerage firm include:

- Whether or not the broker streams real-time quotes.

- The speed of execution for claims.

- The availability of bank wire services.

- The availability of monthly statements.

- How confirmations are done, whether written or electronic.

Commissions and Other Fees

Commission fees are paid when an options trader enters and exits positions. Every brokerage firm has its commission fees set up. These are typically developed around the level of account activity and account size of the options trader.

These are not the only fees that an option trader needs to consider when considering brokerage firms. Many brokerage firms charge penalty fees for withdrawing funds and not maintaining minimum account balances—the existence of fees such as these cuts on any options trader's profit margin. The payment of fees needs to be kept to a minimum to gain maximum income, and as such, an options trader needs to be aware of all fees that exist and how they are applied when operating with a brokerage firm.

Broker Reputation and Options Expertise

Therefore, you must choose a broker that has an established and long-standing reputation for trading options. You also want to deal with a brokerage firm that has great customer service, that can aid in laying the groundwork for negotiating reduced commissions and allows for flexibility. Options trading is a complex service, and your brokerage firm needs to be able to provide support when you are handling difficult transactions.

A list of reputable online brokerage firms include:

- E*Trade
- OptionsXpress

- Scottrade
- Ameritrade
- Train Station

You can look up any of these brokerage websites and find that they have a long-standing reputation for quality service. Even though most are based in the United States, many accept international accounts.

Power Principle #5 – Ensure that Exits Are Automated

Even though I have stated that emotions should be set aside when trading options, we are all human, and emotions are bound to come into the equation at some point. Knowing this, systems must be developed to minimize the impact of emotions. Having your exits automated is one such step that you can take to ensure that emotions are left out when dealing with options day trading. Using bracket orders facilitates this.

Chapter 25. Trading Cryptocurrencies

Cryptocurrency is quickly growing in popularity. For example, Bitcoin, one of the most popular cryptocurrencies and the very first one, is used just like the regular currencies you use on a day to day basis. Ethereum is more for startups who are trying to enhance the blockchain technology. And many other options are out there, and they are used in different ways.

Since there is a lot of volatility that comes with these markets, which means that once you learn how to work with the charts that each has, you will be able to benefit from the many highs and lows and ups and downs that come with these cryptocurrency markets out there.

We will see some of the different strategies that you can work with to use day trading on cryptocurrency.

Breakout

The breakout procedure is going to revolve around the idea that the cost is going to clear a predetermined dimension in your outline with some expanded volume.

This strategy is going to have the trader go into a long position after the currency breaks above the opposition. Then you will again enter into a short position once you see that the currency breaks underneath it.

Scalping

You will find that scalping is going to work well with this kind of security. There are a lot of trades that occur in this market regularly. People all around the world are always looking to find ways to make more money from these markets, and there is a constant exchange between various other currencies and the cryptocurrency that you want to work with. Scalping will help you to make profits in the process. For this, you will just watch for all the downturns that come with the market, and then you will purchase the currency. Then you will move on to selling it as soon as the price or the value goes up.

Steady Incremental Profit Accumulation Strategy or SIPAS

Assuming that the exchange you are using for the cryptocurrency is going to work with USDT, and all of the major and reputable ones do, the goal for the day is for you to produce at least one to two percent from a few altcoins. You want to make sure that the altcoins have a history of stability over the past two or more days. This is going to help you to produce a profit that is at least 7 percent in 12 hours. If you do this over a week, you can earn more than 50 percent in profits.

Besides, if you can find an altcoin that has been doing some consolidation over the past few days, then this is a good option to go with as well. What we want to make sure we are avoiding here is big fluctuations in the price. Using this simple strategy can make sure that you stay on track and that you will profit from that initial investment in two weeks or less.

It is also possible for you to go for a higher profit than what we are talking about here. This isn't a problem and can be pretty easy, but remember that the bigger the profit you want to earn, the more risk you add to it all. And greed is always going to result in a drain to your profits, regardless of how much knowledge you have about the market and everything else.

For the most part, the one to two per cent increments is the best. If you can stick with these numbers, you will be able to avoid all of the big losses that can occur once the emotions, and a large amount of money is on the line in that particular trade.

There is a lot of volatility that can show up in the market for cryptocurrencies, and it is important to really understand the market, to pick out one that has been relatively stable over the recent time, and then work with that one to do the right day trades that will bring in profit. If you can bring it all together, you will be able to make some good profits in the process.

Forex Trading

The foreign exchange currency market, more commonly written as the forex market, is the largest of all the investment markets, currently boasting more than 4 trillion dollars' worth of transactions per day, or roughly ten times more than what the New York Stock Exchange can manage. Despite the lucrative potential available in this market, it was long outside the realm of the amateur trader as technological limitations made it difficult to amass the information required for such an undertaking.

Before jumping in with both feet, you are going to want to keep in mind the fact that the forex market is completely speculative, which means that unlike in most markets when you buy and sell in the forex market, you aren't gaining anything physical in the process. Another, your gains and losses are then expressed in the currency of your choosing.

If this seems like a bit of an odd system, that's because the forex market only exists because international organizations and countries needed an easy way to move currency around in massive quantities without going through the steps the average person would be required to do such a thing. These entities tend to trade in units of currency that are so extreme they can actually affect the overall value of the currencies being traded, which is where the speculative side of the market comes into play.

Generally speaking, only about 20 percent of the movement in the forex market is from these major entities, with the rest coming from investors that are trying to make a buck from the movement that spreads out through the market as a result. While a majority of these investors are professionals working for financial institutions or hedge funds, more and more private traders are jumping on the bandwagon each year, drawn to the promise of potentially huge wins thanks to the available leverage.

Forex Facts

When the market moves, the smallest amount that is tracked is known as a pip which is one percent of the total price of the currency in question. When you are first starting out in the forex market, you are going to want to avoid taking on trades that are larger than a micro lot as in this case, and the pip is worth 10 cents of the currency you are working with. This means you won't quickly lose your shirt when a trade turns against you at the last moment. If you stray to mini lots or standard lots, you run the risk of losing $1 or $10, respectively, per pip. For reference, you can expect a trending currency to move around 100 pips per trading session.

While the forex market differs from other markets in key ways, it is important to always keep in mind that it is the same in the ways that matter the most as it is driven by supply and demand as much as any other market. This means that when a certain currency is in high demand, then the value of that currency will naturally continue to increase until the point where the market has more sellers than it does buyers. At this point, the price will start to drop until the buyers start to bite once more.

When trading in the forex market, it is extremely important to be aware of instances where a specific currency is about to increase in demand so that you can jump on it as quickly as possible. This means you will want to keep abreast of things like economic predictions related to world powers, current geopolitical strife and key interest rate movements.

While closed on the weekends, during the week, the market naturally shifts its focus between various currency pairs based on the portion of the world that is currently the most active. For example, the currency pair USD/JPY would be active during the portion of the day when the US is active and again when Japan is active. The forex market is divided into three segments based on the time of day in the US, Asia and Europe. This isn't anything that is strictly regulated, as the forex market isn't regulated in any traditional sense. Rather it is simply more profitable to trade a specific currency when it is the most active.

Lack of Traditional Regulation

As already noted, the forex market is not regulated in nearly the same way as other markets and is considered an unregulated exchange. This essentially means that when someone chooses to make a trade dishonestly, they are not going to be at the mercy of any regulatory body, which means it is up to the community to dish out justice. As such, every trade in the forex market is based on what is known as a credit agreement, which essentially means everyone operates in good faith. As anyone who breaks the agreement will never be able to trade in the forex market again, it tends to work fairly well in most instances.

In addition to this system, the US also has what's known as the National Futures Association, which is a voluntary organization that forex dealers can join, which holds its members to a higher standard than the market as a whole. It also offers arbitration options if a disagreement does occur.

As there is no one to enforce such things, the rules are more relaxed in the forex market as well. This means you are free to short sell as much currency as you have access to as long as you think you can make a profit off of it. On the other hand, there is also no limit to how many lots you can buy in a single trade, which means you could make a billion-dollar trade if you had the cash.

Finally, the number of traditional forex brokers are few and far between which means that a majority of forex transactions don't require a commission fee. Rather, forex dealers make their money off of the spread, which means it is likely going to be a bit larger than what you may be used to. This means the forex market is principal only, which means the dealers are taking on just as much risk as the traders.

Conclusion

While the above description might make it sound as although day trade is distinctly straightforward, the reality of the problem is that it's far a very complicated process requiring a hit use of quite a few tools and competencies that not absolutely everyone will be capable of follow thru on reliably.

The largest seasoned on the subject of day trading is the capacity for benefit while the entirety goes in keeping with plan. The typical successful day dealer tends to shop for a large number of stocks at a time to make sure that they stand to make a serious make the most of even a minimal quantity of movement. Additionally, they can work for themselves, most uncomplicated trading, while they experience the urge or when the market is in a place that is too correct to bypass up.

Another significant benefit to day trading for certain forms of buyers is the quantity of excitement they can assume to see on day by day basis. As they handiest ever alternate within the absolute shortest timeframes, the typical day trader sees a long way greater movement than maximum other types of buyers would in the same quantity of time. What's greater, day trading provides people who are up to the undertaking with the opportunity to face off with many of the excellent investors in the world, dozens, if not hundreds of times each day. If you're the sort of thrill-seeker who is sure to appreciate an impressive spike of adrenaline, then day trading might be for you.

Also, day trading is that you may educate yourself as effortlessly as you may pay someone else to teach you what to do, making it one of the few ways you may get a job within the monetary zone with proper education. As lengthy as you're inclined and able to put inside the time and dedicated enough to look it thru to the end, then there may be no reason you may not gather the skills you want on your very own and then hone them via endless hours of practice.

Trading is a mental activity. You don't need to lift or push anything physically. Therefore, it is crucial to ensure that your mental state is as optimal as it needs to be for you to execute properly; having a checklist or a mental check-in list works wonders for the trading process. Aside from that, honing your intuition would help a lot in your process. If you hope to be a successful day trader, then you are going to need to get into the habit of making popular trades before they become popular for the best results.

As such, you need to get into the habit of always following the beat of your drum when it comes to drawing conclusions from your research and acting accordingly. While this doesn't mean listening to your gut if you have put in the time and done the work and it all points in a direction that no one else has gone in yet then you need to be confident enough in your abilities to get in before things turn in that direction. Just for finishing, read and reread this book as many times as you need it because you will find all the essential information to learn and grow in this business. Improve yourself every day and enjoy the process.